MIRACLES
— IN —
THE DARK

How a Childhood Cult and Abuse Survivor
Reclaimed the Light

TAMMY RENÉ

Publishing support provided by
Ignite Press
5070 N. Sixth St. #189
Fresno, CA 93710
www.IgnitePress.us

ISBN: 979-8-9894466-0-5
ISBN: 979-8-9894466-1-2 (E-book)

For bulk purchases and for booking, contact:

Tammy René
915tammy@gmail.com
buildonthelight.com

The names of certain individuals have been changed to respect their privacy.

Trigger Warning: This book contains material of a highly sensitive nature including mentions of sexual abuse
that may be triggering for some individuals.

Library of Congress Control Number: 2023919897

Cover design by K M Shahidul Arafat
Edited by Elizabeth Arterberry
Interior design by Jetlaunch

FIRST EDITION

WHAT PEOPLE ARE SAYING ABOUT
MIRACLES IN THE DARK

Miracles in the Dark is a riveting story that affirms that "only when we are brave enough to explore the darkness will we discover the infinite power of our light (Brené Brown)." It testifies to the strengthening power to endure and prevail over life's greatest adversities through faith in our Savior, Jesus Christ, who is intimately aware of the details of our lives. *Miracles in the Dark* will inspire you to use your God-given gift of free agency, to choose hope rather than despair, and to ultimately determine your destiny.

Tammy's courage to vulnerably explore the darkness that engulfed her youth enabled the discovery of her divine identity. She exemplifies a strong woman who discovered the infinite power of her light and overcame great physical and emotional abuse to find joy. Tammy's compassion, love, and the beautiful light that radiates from within her are felt by those who are fortunate enough to know her.

Diane Covington,
Registered Nurse/Medical Research Expert

When I started reading Tammy's book, I was in awe of the trauma she had endured, and I was so captivated by her story of overcoming the dark experiences of her past. This book is a very special one. It is gripping, heart-wrenching, and filled with light. I believe that everyone who reads it will be better able to heal from their own difficult memories by going on this journey with Tammy and utilizing the array of helpful tools she discovered. Ultimately, the book is one of hope and healing. It touched me deeply and the story has stayed with me.

Nancy Jones,
M.A. American Studies, Founder of *Sweetly Sings Stickers*

Miracles in the Dark is just that, the story of miraculous life being created from the darkness. I have known Tammy's story in pieces for many years, but to read about it, was heartbreaking, and uplifting. Seeing God's power in her life and knowing that the Lord can provide that miracle of light to others who need it is the miraculous part. What God can do that none other is capable of is healing, true, miraculous healing, from things that the world tells us we are not able to heal from. Forgiveness is the key she unlocks for everyone from relaying her experiences in the dark closet to blossoming into the light of Jesus. Read this book and be mesmerized by her transformation only possible in one place, a place of faith.

Jeanne Koerner,
Realtor, Podcaster: *Living Your Best Authentic Life*

To my husband, for his compassion, understanding, and strength in walking this journey together

To my children and grandchildren for helping me see outside myself

To friends and family along the way who share their light

and
To the hurting children inside each of us—may they reclaim their light and live the beautiful life waiting for them.

PRESENCE OF SENSITIVE CONTENT

This personal account of overcoming great hardship and duress contains content and themes some may find upsetting or difficult to handle, such as physical, sexual, and ritual abuse of minors. This content is not presented in an unnecessarily graphic manner, only meant to serve the reader in understanding the author's experiences and in honestly and completely displaying the most challenging aspects of healing from trauma. There are also mentions of threats of suicide and depictions of precarious mental states, though, again, these details are relayed in the interest of transparency and accuracy in relaying the author's lived experience and journey to healing.

TABLE OF CONTENTS

FOREWORD

Dear Reader,

When I started my practice in 1975 as a licensed Ph.D. Marriage and Family Therapist, I felt like I was well trained and prepared for the challenge. What I was not prepared for was the amount and frequency of abuse I would deal with for the next forty-five years. When I first started to deal with molestation and ritual abuse, it was hard for me to believe that human beings, especially those close to the person, could be so cruel and inhumane. I now, for sure, am no longer surprised at the evil that can be and is perpetrated on innocent victims.

This book is not an easy read. My hope is that those who have not had the kinds of painful experiences you will read about herein will have a better understanding of those who have. Furthermore, I feel that those who have experienced abuse in their lives may be able to receive hope from Tammy's journey. I have few heroes in my life, but those who, like Tammy and her husband, have had the courage and fortitude to fight the hard fight and come out better, stronger, and healthier, are heroes to me. I commend her journey to you and wish her, and you, a good life.

Cordially,
D. Wayne Abbott, Ph.D.

SECTION ONE

THE JOURNEY

CHAPTER 1

THE GARDENER

Terror. That's really the only word that describes the intense helplessness and fear that shadowed me throughout my youth and childhood. At four and five years old, I was terrified of the night—fearful of what Dad would do to me at night when Mom wasn't home and fearful of Mom's tirades and abuse on the nights she didn't work. Each night, I laid frozen under the covers of the bed I shared with my two sisters. On the nights the terror could not be quieted, I snuck into the closet and hid among the dirty clothes and broken toys.

One night, while in my closet, I hugged my knees to my chest as an uneasy sleep gave way to a beautiful dream. Suddenly, the holey t-shirt that I slept in became a flowy dress the color of yellow daffodils. I stood on the top of a hill covered with grass and wildflowers and soaked in soft sunlight. At the bottom of the hill, water danced down a sparkling creek bed, sending its song over the sweet and earthy meadows.

I wandered through the flowers, caressing their petals and breathing in their honey-citrus aroma. Then I saw him. A man dressed in loose-fitting, light-colored clothes was kneeling in the grass, tending colorful flower beds near the creekbank. I watched for a moment, a little afraid of going closer. The sunlight seemed to gather around him; the sight touched something peaceful in my heart and made me feel safe—I wanted to be near him. I weaved my way down the hill through the colorful flowers and watched as he carefully inspected each leaf and bud, gently pulling the few weeds growing at the flower's roots. Beside him was a wooden bucket full of water. He dipped a ladle into the bucket and offered each flower a life-giving drink. There was a soft kindness about him that washed away my fears. I moved closer.

After a moment, he looked at me with eyes full of color, smiled, and offered me a drink of the same clear water. Its coolness almost tasted sweet and quenched an unknown thirst deep within me. He rose and led me to a bench on the edge of the creek. We talked without words. When it was time for me to go, he gave me a hug and said, "Everything will be okay." The love I felt in that moment pushed past my pain and pierced the deep, empty, and haunted parts of my heart.

My Gardener Dream came to me often in my youth and strengthened the barrier between the dark trauma of my home life and me, but shadows of the acts that should only happen in nightmares remained. For years, I desperately searched for a light big enough to make the shadows disappear. Time moved forward, and the nightmarish memories inside grew too big to stay hidden. About the time of my thirty-first birthday, the barrier that protected the light in my life from the dark and haunting trauma cracked like an earthquake fractures a foundation. Images of my Gardener came to the forefront; I prayed for light and received truth.

I prayed for light and received truth.

CHAPTER 2

TIDAL WAVE

"And ye shall know the truth, and the truth shall make you free."

John 8:32 (KJV)

M y thirty-first birthday came and went, and for the first time in my life, I was mostly feeling good about who I was—or at least, who I thought I was.

My husband, Eric*, and I had a full life with our five children: Chance*, Lori*, Shane*, Cali*, and Amy* (*name has been changed). Eric and I met at college thirteen years earlier. He was tall, handsome, and we clicked right away; I loved being with him and felt a freedom to be myself for the first time in my life. After a year of dating, we postponed college and married in the fall of 1979. Eric's parents and brother easily welcomed me into the family, and we moved to his hometown to start what looked like an adult life.

The first years of marriage had their struggles. I had to learn to express myself without anger. We both worked to be compassionate through our bad moods, to listen when we would rather be doing something else, and to figure out how to merge our individualities.

We had our fifth child on our ninth wedding anniversary. Each child brought a new kind of love, a new demand on our energies, and more opportunity for learning and growth. Our full house filled the vague, unknown, and haunting emptiness inside me. I was busy and exhausted but grateful for a full schedule to immerse myself in.

I wanted to be the perfect mom and create the perfect home for our family. The thought of failing my children would almost suffocate me at times. I studied other families at our church, looking for role models to help me give my children the best life possible. My lifelong struggle with poor self-esteem pushed me to study about ways to help my children with theirs. The main theory I ran across asserted that consistency and assigned responsibilities were key. Chore charts and lists of daily tasks took on different forms as I struggled to find the perfect formula. Eric and I ran a small business together, using our home for an office. I thrived on the full schedule and found a new inner strength in developing organizational skills in both my business and home life. Even with imperfect efforts, I saw progress and my confidence flourished.

Eric was athletic and loved physical activity. As our family grew, he made sure our Saturdays were filled with things like basketball, camping, or boating excursions on one of the nearby lakes. On Sundays, we enjoyed the peace of serving in our local church group and often rested from the hectic week.

Our family found a good rhythm of balancing day-to-day responsibilities with family time. We lived in a brand-new home with large picture windows that overlooked an unfinished backyard and the peace and strength of the beautiful Sierra Nevada mountain range. Our little corner of northern Nevada offered a sense of home I never had growing up.

As much as I loved spending time with my family, personal time was a necessity. Three times a week, at five in the morning, I met my friends to run, talk, and absorb the peaceful moments of the stillness between dark and dawn before our busy schedules took over our existence. The leftover feelings of being an outcast in my youth were dormant. Still, deep inside me, there was darkness and fear. The trouble was, there was no face or name to it all.

The trauma in my childhood was stored deep inside me, trapped behind a concrete barrier thicker, higher, and stronger than Hoover Dam. The more I felt good about my current life and tried to enjoy its light, the more unrest I felt about my past—there was an emptiness inside me regarding my parents. I never had a great relationship with them; by the time I was an adult, our bond felt burdened and forced. Now, the always present, uncomfortable feelings about my parents intensified. I wanted to be a good daughter and love them unconditionally, but the desire to be close to them was vague and abstract. I prayed to have a softened heart.

Their divorce seven years earlier inspired an unexplained sense of relief in me. As much as I felt guilty for not mourning their breakup, I also felt a strange comfort in only having to be around one of them at a time. Questions about how I reacted to their divorce tried to come to the surface, along with an uneasiness about being around either of my parents. Still, the emotional guardian within me kept the secrets trapped behind the dam.

My eyes opened to a deep chasm buried inside me that severed my current life from my childhood.

On my thirty-second birthday, the breaking of the barrier started. Dad called to wish me a happy birthday and the conversation drifted to my eleven-year-old son's birthday, which was coming up in a few short months. Then Dad asked the question that sent me into a tailspin: "Can Chance stay with me this summer to celebrate his twelfth birthday?"

My stomach dropped. I just could not say yes. The thought of Chance alone with Dad started a tidal wave of emotions that slammed against the barrier that protected me from my parents. My eyes opened to a deep chasm buried inside me that severed my current life from my childhood. The thought of building a bridge to span the abyss came to mind for a moment, then disappeared; the barrier was thinning.

In the quiet moments when I washed dishes or picked up toys while the children played outside, the unanswered questions I had since my parents' divorce snuck past the guardian and meandered into my conscious thoughts. Dormant scenes from my childhood came to life, like my brain was scanning the past for something that would not quite come into focus. Images of Dad's naked body flashed in front of me. But that was Dad, he often roamed the house with no clothes on and had my sisters and I take turns helping him with his baths. He was young and did not need help, really; he just liked the company. Back then it was "the norm" in our house; now it just seemed weird.

Thoughts of Dad continued to float in and out of my mind while images of Mom's angry face rose from the past, setting off warning sirens from somewhere near my gut. I shoved those images back behind the barrier, angry that my brain seemed to be trying to make a monster out of Mom. I remembered Mom cried when Dad left her, and how she begged me to be on her side in case he started saying awful things about her. *What awful things would he say and why?* I wondered at the time, believing she was delirious because of the divorce. Now, the whys about Mom's fears haunted me.

Dad quickly married a woman with three girls and a couple of boys. He was giddy about having young girls in his house again. Thoughts of Dad's fourteen-year-old stepdaughter sitting on his lap as he squeezed her leg and teased her about sex crept eerily into my mind. *Was that why his second wife left him?* I wondered.

Sickness, sirens, and panic surged up from the bottom of the chasm. I buried myself in bookwork for my business and took on extra volunteer time at the school, trying to stuff it all back behind the disintegrating dam.

Then, Dad called on a Thursday in mid-November and announced he would be at our house the following morning to celebrate an early Thanksgiving, complete with a turkey dinner. It was a twelve or thirteen-hour drive from his house in northern Arizona to ours, and he planned to stay for the weekend. Frustrated that I had no say in his coming and uninterested in seeing him, I secretly hoped his car would break down on the way to keep him from coming. However, on Friday morning, he showed up uninvited and on time. I did not feel like celebrating but was grateful for a day filled with cooking and eating that required little interaction.

On Saturday, the weather was bad, so we spent most of the day inside with an ominous heaviness in our family room that stifled any activity. Emptiness mixed with a foreboding towards Dad debilitated me; all I could think to do was continue working on a Christmas quilt for my mother-in-law. I stayed busy at my sewing machine on one side of the room while Eric and the children watched more TV than usual on the other side. Eric tried to engage Dad in conversation, but Dad sat in a chair near me. He shifted his attention from the TV to me in the hopes that he could force through the invisible guard between us. His words mixed with the sound of the sewing machine like the white noise of a whirring fan. I responded with "mmm-hmm," "maybe," or "I'm not sure" to his various questions and comments. Sickness in the pit of my stomach churned. This time, I could not even let my guard down to feel guilty; I just focused on Eric's mom's quilt.

Sunday came. Eric and I found a reprieve with the children at church while Dad spent a good part of the day taking care of some type of business at Tahoe. Monday morning, he was gone before we got up. There was a weird stillness in the house while he was there, and we were all relieved when he left.

My thirty-second Christmas was a blur of activity and emotional uneasiness, but I remember being grateful for the new year and getting back into our normal routine. On a quiet February morning, I was home alone with our two youngest children, Cali and Amy; together, we were half-working and half-playing as we cleaned the kitchen. Cali danced her five-year-old self back and forth across the kitchen floor while Amy focused on carefully placing plates on the racks of the dishwasher in toddler-helping excitement. It was a slower-paced day than usual, and I was looking forward to some relaxing down time before the other kids came home from school.

The phone rang. There was no caller ID back then; I wonder now, *If I had known it was Dad, would I have bothered answering?* I dried my hands and answered the call. The sound of Dad's voice on the other end turned my insides upside-down. I closed the dishwasher and, without looking Cali or Amy in the eye, simply pointed to the family room and whispered, "Go play."

I turned back to the kitchen, tied by the length of the telephone cord I now twisted in my fingers.

"How are things at your house today?" Dad asked.

"Okay, I guess. How are you?"

"You'll be happy to hear I'm turning my life around. I've been going to church regularly and feel like a new man."

"That's great," were the only words I could find. My heart tried to be happy at the thought of him getting back on a good path. He had been bitter since his second divorce and maybe something good could come out of this change.

An unexplained confusion clouded my brain during the conversation. I paced back and forth, stopped to get a cookie out of the cookie jar, and half-listened to Dad ramble on while I tried to figure out why I could not be more supportive. The girls rushed over at the sound of the cookie jar lid; I numbly handed each a cookie while I nibbled on another.

"Well, what do you think?" Dad interrupted my thoughts.

There was an awkward silence.

"Oh, I'm sorry, I didn't hear that last part. What do I think about what?"

"I'm getting married again. This time, at the church, and I really want you to be there."

It felt like Dad just dropped a bomb that rocked my very core. *With Dad at church?* Something about the thought of being with him in a sacred place sent my insides spinning. Heck, I had uneasy feelings about being *anywhere* with him, but church? A hurricane started in my stomach.

"You remember me telling you about Karen? We've been dating for a couple of months now."

"Right, she sounds nice." *Who's Karen? Did he already tell me about her?*

"She's great and has two of the cutest little girls," he continued.

The sick sweetness in his voice when he mentioned the little girls spun the hurricane in my stomach out of control until I thought I would heave. My knees buckled; I grabbed onto the kitchen counter to steady myself.

"Well, can you come?"

Another awkward silence.

"Um… Let me talk to Eric."

"You can just come by yourself."

No! A voice screamed in my head while I struggled to get words out of my mouth. "You know what? I'll have to get back to you on that."

The rest of his words blurred, and I hung up the phone, barely able to get out "good-bye." My insides felt flipped out of order. I was ashamed that I did not want to support him in what seemed like a happy thing in his life. *Why am I having this weird reaction?*

In the next few weeks, the troubling feelings continued to resurface. Something felt wrong. I was doing so well in so many areas of my life, why was I having these uneasy feelings towards my dad? Why couldn't I just love him?

I prayed earnestly to see my earthly father as Heavenly Father sees him. Prayer made me confident that my uneasiness would disappear and I could learn to be a more loving daughter. But as I continued to pray for a healing in my feelings towards my dad, a deep awareness woke up inside me. Pictures from my childhood haunted me like still-life photos, challenging me to remember the rest of a forgotten story, that story protected and firmly held behind concrete-and-steel walls. Something was missing.

The uneasiness about my dad gnawed at me. Dark images hung ghost-like in the background as I contemplated my life and childhood and wondered why the haunting feelings about my father could not be resolved.

On a clear spring day, while Eric was at work and the older children were at school, I put Cali and Amy down for naps and determined to put all the chaos in my brain on paper in hopes of seeing everything more clearly. Focus escaped me. In my search for peace, I picked up a gospel-based magazine and flipped through the pages. A sketch of a young girl caught my eye. Inset into the picture was a quote from the article it accompanied: "It is only now that I am recognizing that scared, angry little girl, crouching in a corner of my soul."[1]

My heart stopped for a moment, and an agonizing cry rose from somewhere deep inside me. The words *my dad did something horrible to me* thundered through my head as a storm tore through my insides. Over and over came the words: *Dad did something horrible to me.*

Trembling, I called Eric at work, crying but not able to explain. He asked where Amy and Cali were, and I reassured him they were okay and napping. He promised to come right home. Slow minutes passed while the storm inside me pushed hard against my chest. The concrete of the dam swayed, and a tidal wave of agony threatened to explode all the barriers. Finally, Eric was there and held me as I sobbed uncontrollably.

> *It is only now that I am recognizing that scared, angry little girl, crouching in a corner of my soul.*

Painful pictures of my dad sexually molesting me came into focus, causing an explosion that ripped my world into a million pieces. I struggled to put it all into words as Eric listened, his strong arms holding me tightly. The concrete-and-steel walls of protection burst. Floodgates opened and the tidal wave rushed to the surface as the previously still pictures came to life and flooded into the present. Then, in the middle of the chaos, a wave of relief rushed over me, under me, around me, and through me. I began to see the truths: the scary secrets buried deep behind the walls that my Guardian built to protect me.

Unsure of how to handle what was going on with me, Eric called the local volunteer leader of our church to see if he could give us some direction on where to go for help. He invited us to come visit with him at his office and the hurricane inside me quieted. This leader also happened to be a medical doctor, and he shared with us that he had heard of people bottling up old emotions and memories and that, sooner or later, it all must be dealt with. He referred me to Dr. Abbott, a marriage and family therapist, and we called to make an appointment. Dr. Abbott had a good reputation for marriage and family therapy, and for promoting stress management and life-balance. We hoped he could point me in the right direction.

Several days before the appointment, I started to have very mixed emotions about the whole thing. I had never been to a therapist, psychologist, or psychiatrist before. Some days it felt like I was making a big deal out of nothing. Other times, the tidal waves roared inside me again, spewing ugly images of my childhood and ripping me in two.

Overall, I just wanted to go to my appointment, get some answers, and have it over with. I expected one of two things: either he would tell me I was too stressed and give me a plan to overcome it, or he would just look at me weird, tell me I was crazy, and put me on medication. I was wrong on both counts.

Dr. Abbott was a tall, confident man. He welcomed Eric and me with a smile and a firm handshake as he invited us into his cozy office. Eric and I sat next to each other on a couch. Dr. Abbott sat down in the recliner across from us. "What can I do for you?"

I squirmed in my chair, forcing a smile. "I don't know—I feel fine now. I just get emotional sometimes; it's probably all nothing. I'm sorry, I probably don't even need to be here."

"Well, since we are here, maybe we should just visit," he smiled.

I kind of froze. "I don't know what to say…"

"Why don't you start with what happened that brought you here today?"

After an awkward silence, Eric squeezed my hand. I breathed in and said a little prayer in my heart, searching for a place to start.

"Um, my Dad called a while back and wanted me to go to the church for his wedding." I rambled on about how good it was for Dad to be starting over and how I wanted to be supportive.

Heaviness filled my chest and the now familiar storm roared to life. "I think my Dad did something horrible to me."

I broke out in a cold sweat and shook uncontrollably as pictures flashed through my mind. Sickness rumbled through me with the images that followed. I did not want to see any more and tried to shut off all the ugly images, but they would not go away.

Full memories came. The storm raged as I struggled to tell Dr. Abbott about the emotion and pictures whirling through me. The memory of my dad's touch made me ill, and I was repulsed by the feelings in my own body. I drew in deep breaths, trying to stop the deluge drowning life as I knew it.

"How could it be true?" As the question came out of my mouth, the screaming from inside started all over again as if something inside refused to let me forget it again. No amount of reasoning could turn back the torrent.

After an hour, I recalled the pieces of five or six different memories. The session was done, but I sobbed uncontrollably, my arms crossed in front of me and hands tight around my shoulders, rocking back and forth.

Dr. Abbott stood and put a gentle hand on my shoulder. He apologized that he had another appointment, but suggested Eric and I go get something to eat and come back in an hour. Eric held me tight and led me out the back way. Everything between the two sessions was a blur. I couldn't eat and the hour went by too slow. As we reentered Dr. Abbott's office, my knees buckled and dry heaves rocked my trembling body. Eric wrapped his arm around my waist and helped me back to the couch. No one said a word.

I forced gulps of air down to halt the heaves. My heart quieted and my breath came more easily. Finally, I looked around and saw the pictures on the walls for the first time. I sat up straight and looked Dr. Abbott straight in the eye. "My dad sexually molested me."

The truth was out. The storm dissipated, the water stilled, and quiet filled my insides. The first tidal wave was over.

Dr. Abbott suggested writing to purge myself of the old images and emotion. In the quiet aftermath of that first visit, it did not seem necessary. A reprieve came as I went through the motions of "normal" life and I felt that, surely, I had reached the light at the end of the tunnel. The days passed, but there was an emptiness in me where there used to be a happy satisfaction. It was like there was a wormhole inside that sucked the energy out of me. When I tried to rest, the dormant scenes of my childhood came to life again, bringing waves of sickening emotion with them. I gave in and purchased a small notebook, expecting to fill it up in a few weeks and move on.

As I allowed the memories to come, the walls that kept them hidden crumbled. More images of Dad molesting me came to the surface, proving it was a pattern that continued throughout my childhood. Pictures of Mom hurting me also moved in and out of the scenes coming to life. The hate in her eyes burned through my heart and the old indistinct fear of her rumbled inside.

It helped to have a notebook as a dumping ground for the emotions that plagued me. Allowing myself to feel at all was a monumental task. It felt like if I let all the feelings inside me out, it would literally kill me, that the pain would be so intense I would never recover.

Eric and I did not want to poison our current life with the past, so I tried to keep it all in my notebook and hold the waves of emotion back by attempting regular life. The stormwaters raged inside me until it was almost impossible to hold it all in until my weekly visits with Dr. Abbott. Desperate to be done with it all, I started spending more and more time writing about the memories that plagued me. I immersed myself in capturing the details of my childhood; household chores went undone, volunteer time at the school ended, and business paperwork piled up. My life careened out of the careful pattern I had set and left me engulfed in a long-forgotten but familiar agony.

Late one afternoon, I sat in my room writing exhaustively for several hours. I did not realize how immersed I was until the sound of our children laughing and playing in the backyard jerked me into the present for a moment. When I got up to look out the window, the pent-up storm whirled out of control into a full-blown hurricane. The room spun and turned my legs into Jell-O. Chills pricked my skin while an overwhelming urge to hide sent me stumbling into my closet. I collapsed to the floor, hugged my knees to my chest, and sobbed uncontrollably in the darkness.

"Tammy?" I did not recognize Eric as he opened the door, letting a sliver of light into the dark abyss.

It felt like my 5'7" frame had disappeared into the body of a thin, mousy-brown-haired five-year-old huddled in the dirty closet of my childhood. A bolt of terror shot through me, forcing a childlike voice to the surface. "Daddy, please don't hurt me again."

Eric knelt and held my hand; his tender voice assured me that I would not be hurt anymore. The safety of the present eased my anguish, bringing me gently forward into my adult self.

Exhaustion deflated me. Eric helped me to bed and went to check on the children. I could hear him in the backyard asking who wanted pizza for dinner. Squeals of excitement mixed with "Oh yeah!" and "Yes!" floated into my room as I closed my eyes and tried to rest; I was grateful to hear Eric playing with the children like there was nothing wrong at all. Sleepiness overtook me and images came of the old house my parents moved into the year before I started kindergarten. I saw myself hiding in the small closet with the dirty clothes and broken toys once again. The closet walls melted away and all around me were grass covered hills soaked in soft sunlight. I turned my face to the cloudless sky and was thirty-two again, taking in the caressing warmth of the light-filled Garden.

> *The safety of the present eased my anguish, bringing me gently forward into my adult self.*

And there He was. My Gardener took my hand, and, together, we followed a brown ribbon path, weaving through giant, leafy oak trees and tiny blooms of pink, yellow, and red. Water danced over stones in the creek that flowed beside us as it blended its music with the voice of the meadowlarks in the distance. Quietly, we walked, and I breathed in the light-filled air, feeling the strength of my Gardener's hand. The pain of dark times retreated as I lost myself in the Gardener's wondrous world. Courage snuck its way into my heart.

The doorbell woke me from my half-asleep state, and a strange peace surrounded me. I thought of Eric and the closet and felt like a little girl. Eric had seen the damaged me and did not walk away. The chasm inside me was bridged, for just a moment, and there was strength in knowing that I was not alone.

The sound of everyone gathering around the table for pizza woke the rest of me to the present. The storms inside paused, and so did the desire to hide. Taking a deep breath, I went in to be with my family, grateful for the light-hearted chatter and the return of my appetite. Our ten-year-old daughter, Lori, reported on something new she learned at school and asked me a question. Fumbling for an answer, I looked up from my pizza and froze. *When was the last time I actually looked her in the eye? How long has it been since I have really seen any of my children?*

With five days remaining until my next appointment with Dr. Abbott, I put my notebook in the drawer of my nightstand and worked to turn my attention back to my current life. At first, it was freeing to make beds, do the dishes, and file business paperwork, but I still napped more than usual, sometimes dozing on the couch while the kids watched Duck Tales on TV. Exhaustion teased from behind the curtain of attempted normalcy.

The day before my appointment, new hauntings came and stirred the quiet storms back to life. The sense of freedom was gone and my old skill of being able to stuff everything away vanished. There was still a hurt little girl inside that needed to be healed.

⇥ INTO THE LIGHT ⇤

The reality that I was severely abused by my parents turned my life upside down. It threw me into a world I wasn't sure I wanted to be in, but, even during the bouts of denial, there was a relief in having the truth come out.

> **"Extensive international research on psychological trauma and evidence-based treatments of PTSD provides a solid ground for knowledge and a method to help survivors recover. Healing means expressing memories of traumatic experiences and constructing a personal narrative of past, present, and future. It also means defining the biopsychosocial effects—effects which live in a survivor's present experience.** *A research pioneer in the field, Bessel Van der Kolk states that 'in order to heal, you need to know and feel what you feel.' Recovery can lead to finding a meaning and to post-traumatic growth.* **This is true for all of us. After all, underneath, we are all the same."** *— Mary Beth Williams, PhD, LSCW, CTS & Soili Poijula, PhD, The PTSD Workbook, Third Edition*

When I was ready to address it, I found that there is a freedom in allowing ourselves to feel and express the intense emotions linked to our trauma. As we discover ways to express and let go of those emotions with professional guidance and counseling, a sense of peace can accompany the process.

CHAPTER 3

THE INNER CHILD

Reverting to my five-year-old self in my closet scared me. Part of me was ashamed I was such a mess, and part of me was worried that I was broken beyond repair. This time, my session with Dr. Abbott was different. I told him about the closet and about my Gardener dream.

"What's going on with me?" was my only question.

First, he corrected the misguided (but well-intended) advice from our church leader that told us we should not discuss the hard things during the week but save them for our appointments with Dr. Abbott to guide us through them. He explained, "That often works for people in marriage counseling, but the reason it may not work for you is that for your whole life, you had to keep the secrets inside—it was your burden to carry. A major part of your healing has to come from letting those secrets out and allowing yourself to not be alone."

"A major part of your healing has to come from letting those secrets out and allowing yourself to not be alone."

He suggested limiting my writing to an hour a day and that I share those things with Eric or any trusted friend. "Put fear aside and trust your instincts about it."

Dr. Abbott explained that the traumatic events of my childhood were frozen in storage in the recesses of my brain. It is a built-in safety mechanism that keeps us functioning on some level during the most harrowing of times. It is like what happens to war veterans, such as those who served in Vietnam. Many of the most horrific experiences are kept hidden from the conscious mind until the victim is in a somewhat emotionally safe place. It is called post-traumatic stress disorder. When the victim is ready, those events come to the surface to be dealt with or processed. For me, the dark experiences were largely kept boxed away so the light could gain my focus. Basically, for the first thirty-two years of my life, I was mentally incapable of dealing with the extent of the trauma inflicted by my parents.

The PTSD theory was reinforced for me when I experienced the very real sensation of being five years old again, scared and hiding on the floor of our closet while Eric held me. For me, it was not only the memories, pain, and fear that had been hidden away, it was like there were actual parts of me that had been boxed away as well. I was not whole. Even with the beautiful beams of light scattered throughout my experiences, I was broken into a puzzle of a thousand pieces with only a handful visible. Now, it seemed the Lord was placing boxes on my path that contained the long-lost pieces of me. *Could the brokenness really be healed?* The idea that there were parts of me that needed healing instead of feeling like I was hopelessly "crazy" rekindled my motivation. And so, I continued to write, pray, and struggle to move forward.

Writing about each painful image and allowing myself to shed the pent-up tears brought relief. I felt sure that as I accepted the realities that faced me, the end of the trauma would come; I could move on with "normal" life and put this all behind me. Weeks passed. The small notebook was filled, and I reluctantly bought another.

Somewhere in the middle of all the remembering, Dad called. His voice startled me. I had avoided the reality that at some point I would have to confront him. My shocked silence was interrupted by Dad's questions about why he hadn't heard from me and when Chance would be coming for the summer.

The truth rumbled inside me. "He won't be coming. I know what you did."

Eric came to stand beside me.

"What do you mean?" Dad asked.

"I know you sexually molested me when I was a child." A shaky strength punctuated my words.

Silence.

After a moment, his voice got sticky sweet, "Ah, poor little Tammy—always afraid of the boogie man. Do you really think I would do those things to a scared, weak little girl?"

His words struck a weird chord. Suddenly I felt weak, small, and scared.

"Yes, I do." I shook all over as light was released inside me.

His voice lowered. "If you know what's good for you, you better leave the past alone."

No denial, no remorse.

Hot tears burned my eyes and the shaky strength stabilized. I didn't know how to respond, so I simply handed Eric the phone, went into the family room, flopped on the couch, and closed my eyes to my children's laughter as they enjoyed some silly TV show.

After the phone call, Eric and I talked. He said that he told Dad, "It's all coming out now, everything you did." Dad got angry at him and told him none of it was his business and that, even if we tried to tell anyone, no one would believe us. Once again, no denial. On the outside, I was frozen in place, while, inside, the storms swirled around a growing confidence that the things I remembered were real.

A small window of peace broke through the turmoil.

Eric took my hands—he told me he did not want any of us to have anything to do with my dad anymore. My first thought, maybe more like a vague hope, was, *What if Dad repents? Everything would be better, right?* For now, though, I knew this was the right decision. A small window of peace broke through the turmoil.

Until that day, it was difficult to find the courage to talk to my sisters about what was going on, and I had no desire to communicate with Mom at all. After confronting Dad, it felt like the once-barricaded doors opened, and it was time to be bold.

I called my older sister, Leah* (*name has been changed), and stumbled through explanations of what I was remembering. She said she didn't have time to talk but told me I shouldn't be so worried about the past. The call ended abruptly. I wondered if she knew something she did not want to talk about or simply thought I was crazy.

The call to my younger sister, Sadie* (*name has been changed), was different. After a vague explanation about remembering being abused, there was a dead silence on the other end of the phone.

"Sadie? Are you okay?"

Still silence.

"Are you there?"

She finally answered, her voice quiet and shaky, "Yeah, I'm here."

Another pause.

"It's just that lately I've had these dreams…"

"What kind of dreams?" Honestly, the first thought that came to my mind was that she dreamt of me being in a straitjacket in some asylum.

"Well, they're about Dad and… You know what, they're just dreams. I don't want to talk about it."

I did not press the issue. She asked if I was okay. I reassured her that there was peace that accompanied the remembering process. A bolt of strength steadied me in the sharing.

I continued to write, determined to get to the end of this remembering chapter and back to normal life. But as I wrote about the strangling effects of Dad's molestations, images of an old, abandoned house emerged, bringing with it the details of another dark memory. A small glow came from its windows, casting shadows on the cars and trucks parked in the dirt around the building. I was five years old and had never felt so strongly that I didn't want to go inside a place. Dad took me by the hand and, without a word, led me through the door.

There were about twenty men and a few children in the one big room. Some had black robes on already, while others were in the process of quietly changing out of their regular clothes. Dad did the same. Then, he turned to me and, without a word, took off the hole-y nightshirt and panties I came in and slipped a black sheet over my shoulders. Faint meows from a few cats hiding in the corner pierced the silence

Memories of the dark meeting swept through my brain like tornado-force winds: the calculated torture of children and animals. The candle flames cast shadows on the walls that looked like demons dancing with delight at the horrific sights they witnessed. In the sick, silent center of the tornado were images of the twisted and terrifying sexual abuse we children suffered at the hands of each man present.

I wrote the details of the meeting and tried to describe the tremendous fear and pain that came back to me in full force. Vague images of more satanic meetings hung in the background. The emotion was too much; I put the notebook and pen away and sought refuge in cleaning the kitchen while my children continued to play in the backyard.

A love-hate relationship developed between me and my notebook. Days passed. Focusing on housework, business, and fun did not change the haunting images that plagued my waking hours. The demons inside needed to be faced, but I struggled to write. It felt like putting these new memories on paper would make them too real. Instead of words, I doodled flowers and lightning bolts.

One night, I had dreams of falling into a big, black hole, kicking at the darkness and grabbing for something to hold onto. My heart raced at the black-robed memories. Images of the fear-filled dark made my insides tremble. So many pieces of me were trapped in pain and fear. Part of me hoped it was all my imagination, while the rest of me just wanted answers.

Late the next morning, the house was quiet, but my brain wasn't. I knew I needed to pick up my pen and write. Twisting open the blinds, I looked out at the mountains, hoping to breathe in their strength. *Let's get this over with.*

I stood up straighter, walked back to the bedroom, took my notebook from the nightstand, flopped on the bed, and began to write. My mind flashed forward to my preteen years, to haunting pictures of black robes in night-cloaked wilderness. Dark tones rose from the shadow and, once again, a frightened uneasiness worked its way up from the deepest parts of my soul.

A few days later my sister, Sadie, called. She shared memories with exact details from ones I had recalled—only I had never divulged the details of any of them to her. It was strengthening to have the validation that these things were not figments of my imagination.

Not long after that, Mom phoned. "I'm worried about you, why didn't you call me?"

It turns out Sadie had told her about my remembering. Mom said she knew what I was saying was true, but she was too scared of my dad to admit it before.

> *As I wrote, I became aware that it was not the images that demanded my attention, but broken parts of me that begged to be healed.*

"You should be scared, too. You need to call me and let me know anything else you remember."

That last statement felt more like a threat than an attempt at comfort. Her voice twisted my insides.

Keeping my heart and mind open to the contents of the foreboding boxes inside me was tough. I tried to escape through playing with my children and going on mountain hikes with friends, but the images from the boxes of darkness forced their way to the surface, demanding to be acknowledged.

As I wrote, I became aware that it was not the images that demanded my attention, but broken parts of me that begged to be healed.

Pain, anguish, and soul-wrenching cries drove me to my knees. I prayed for relief—for help understanding what this all meant and what I should do with it. At my next appointment,

Dr. Abbott told me about a book, *Homecoming*, by John Bradshaw. It contained instructions and meditations for the reader to get in touch with their "inner child." The goal was to find what the hurt parts of me needed, and bring them into the present to heal. It was a frightening thought. I didn't want the demons that the other parts of me carried to poison the present.

When I told Dr. Abbott my fears, he leaned forward until my eyes met his. "Tammy, if you saw a little girl on the street, bruised and broken, would you really turn her away?"

In the quiet moment that followed, the images of my younger self softened. *I can do this.* Hope urged me forward.

The next day, I took Cali and Amy to the library, excited to check out my life-changing book while the girls were just as excited for *Corduroy* and *Oh, the Places You'll Go.* At home, we snuggled on the couch and enjoyed the colorful pictures and fun word journey of the books they chose. For just a moment, my heart was still. The storms inside me ceased and I was simply a mother, enjoying the warm sunshine of the day and the miracle of my own children's laughter.

For the first time in a long time, nap time for the girls did not need to be nap time for me. I quickly cleared the toys from a living room chair and settled in to read my book and start planning how I was going to heal. Some of the author's ideas seemed a little quack-y. I just could not get on board with the concept that every quirk, weakness, or trial can be completely blamed on our parents or childhood. Still, the theory that the hurt carried inside me could be healed was the food my ravished soul had been seeking, so I continued to read. An actual method for healing the "inner child" energized me in my quest to somehow put the broken pieces of myself back together.

The theory is that the subconscious holds the unresolved pieces of the past that are poisoning the present. Those pieces are held by the hurt child inside who is waiting for healing. By revisiting those moments, you can, as an adult, offer the comfort and help that a child needs to heal, and invite them forward to enjoy the present. The method consists of first getting in touch with the different phases of your childhood by writing about where you lived and the details of that place and time in your life.

Instead of starting with the infant stage and working my way up, I started with the preschool years. It was the five-year-old in me that was begging to be heard. And so, I began to write the details I remembered from that part of my life.

Floating through the pictures of my childhood, I could see the purple mulberry stains on the sidewalk in front of our small cinder block house, the weed-filled front yard, and could almost feel the hot, heavy Phoenix air. The gray of the cinder blocks, the goat-head stickers in the front yard, and the bittersweet taste of the mulberries came into focus. Across the street, a large hill dotted with desert shrub, cactus, and an occasional hackberry tree defied the busy city surrounding it. It was an odd thing on the edge of this old, small-house neighborhood.

My older sister, Leah, was a natural explorer, and when we were just five and six years old, she talked me into daring expeditions up the trail that wound around the hill up to the top. Although she was only a year older than me, I looked up to her as a protector and confidently followed her on the winding paths. We found prickly pear cactus plants that had yellow and pink blossoms in the spring and lizards too fast to catch before they disappeared among the boulders.

As I wrote about our little house and the hill, dormant scenes from my childhood sprang to life. I could almost see myself dancing on the sidewalk singing my brains out to a song I heard a hundred times on our little transistor radio. "Dizzy, my head is spinnin' like a whirlpool it never ends…"

Suddenly, I was in the living room of that little house alone with my sisters, singing and dancing to Mom's new album *Meet the Beatles.* "I Wanna Hold Your Hand" blared while we used broom handles for microphones and an old tennis racket for a guitar.

Music was freedom. Singing and moving my body to the music put me into another world. Our living room transformed into the dance floor of "American Bandstand," a popular music and dance show. Burdens lifted as the fun and beautiful parts of my life unfolded on the page.

And then the music stopped. Suddenly, I was my five-year-old self, wide-eyed and lips trembling, sitting on the edge of my mom's bed while Mom paced back and forth in front of me.

"You talk like a baby. Babies can't go to school. Now say it again."

I took a deep breath and tried again.

"Tweeet."

She slapped me hard across my face; the impact burned my cheek and shoved my head sideways.

"Don't be stupid. Say Sssstreet."

I tried twisting my tongue in a new way, struggling to get the S out, "Tttweeet."

She grabbed my face and leaned over me and turned my face to hers; her fiery brown eyes shot arrows directly into mine. I wanted to say "street;" I wanted Mom to be happy, but the right sound just wouldn't come out. My tummy trembled and tears that wanted to fall stung my eyes.

"You will say it right or so help me…" She stepped back and slapped me again.

I sunk further into despair each time I tried but failed to get the right sounds out. After what felt like hours, Mom left. I sat alone on her bed for a long while, not knowing what she wanted me to do.

My pen stopped. *Why am I writing about such stupid things? It's no big deal.*

More memories of being five rushed forward, bringing all the fear and confusion back with them. I could see little five-year-old me, hurt and scared, hiding in that messy closet. The pain of Dad's molestations and the hate in Mom's eyes broke through barriers, opening my heart to the innocence stolen from my younger self.

For the first time, I felt compassion towards myself. In my youth and young adulthood, that memory evoked regret and shame about not being able to do something so simple. Now, it opened floodgates of sadness and a desire to hold and cradle the little me who tried so hard to be good enough.

The next step in the book's healing process was to write a letter to the younger self you found. I turned the page and wrote, "Dear Tammy, you are beautiful and lovable." Walls crumbled and I wanted more than anything to reach out and comfort the little girl I remembered; to sing "I Wanna Hold Your Hand" and dance with her across the living room floor. I wanted to take her out of that somber, gray house and bring her into the sunshine. Words flowed onto the paper and love filled my heart. "There is a beautiful life waiting for you," I wrote. It felt like a door in my heart opened and there was a new sense of quiet inside.

The second part of the letter-writing was to think of the inner child and imagine what they would write back. Using my non-dominant hand, I began to write. It seemed like the five-year-old in me was a complete and separate person that had been locked away in the darkness within me. As I wrote, I felt that little girl plead to join me in the present. I added a promise to my letter that soon I would come get her.

> *A door in my heart opened and there was a new sense of quiet inside.*

The event was so real it calmed my soul; I was determined to go through with the next step of a self-guided meditation as soon as Eric got home. Amy and Cali's voices and the sounds of them playing in their room carried down the hall. This session was done, and I replaced writing with sitting at the table next to my two little girls and their crayons and coloring books. A spark of child-like creativity woke inside me. Maybe the little five-year-old hiding in the closet wasn't so far from the present after all.

When the older children got home from school, we played Uno instead of tackling our usual chore and homework routine. Cali entertained us all with her nonstop chatter, Shane smiled and rearranged his cards. Chance and Lori kept each other in check by making sure the right cards were placed and the reverses honored. Four-year-old Amy and I were a team, and she insisted that she hold our cards and that I only help her with the numbers. My heart felt unburdened for a small moment.

That evening, after hot dogs and mac 'n' cheese for dinner and family prayer, Eric and I sent the children to bed. We settled in our room to review the day and start on the next phase of my healing—the self-guided meditation.

I read aloud the letter I wrote to my five-year-old self and felt the distance between her and my adult self swallowed up in a hopeful connection. Then Eric guided me through the steps to let go of current worries and, then, I pictured my childhood home and visualized going inside. Part of me fought going back in time, telling myself this was an impossible and stupid idea, but as Eric continued voicing kind affirmations of the love and strength I possess, the fight subsided and left me with only thoughts of the hurt little girl in that house.

Suddenly, the door was opened, and it felt like I was really walking through the front door, down the short hall, and into the room I shared with my sisters. A heavy stillness halted time, and, without effort, the closet door opened and there—shivering in the far corner—was little Tammy. Pain and sadness twisted my gut. Sorrow for this hurt little girl ignited a love I had not felt before. I reached forward, repeating words of promises to protect and love her, and that she would never need to hide in a closet again.

The embrace was not physical, but was like being enveloped in the warmth of a steady fire, melding the little girl and me into one beautiful, whole woman. Warmth and light radiated from deep within my soul and pulsed continually for minutes that seemed like hours.

Sorrow for this hurt little girl ignited a love I had not felt before.

That night, the constant storms in my head were quieted by the love and light that continued to radiate through my whole body. The dream of my Gardener came to mind, and I could almost feel the joy of sitting with him on that bench as I listened to the twinkling brook and embraced the beauty all around us. I wanted to share that joy with my children and wondered if any of them had Garden dreams during their deepest sleep.

⇥ INTO THE LIGHT ⇤

Acknowledging the pain we have been through is the first step in healing—and it can be the scariest. Writing about it is a way to allow the pain an outlet and connect the hurting part of ourselves with the present.

> **"Healing through the written word happens when people learn about themselves and open themselves to the healing power within...By writing about these experiences, these individuals are able to shift the power of the event from the event or experience itself into their own hands."** — *Karen Cangialosi, MFA, MA, Healing Through the Written Word*

Uncovering the most hurt part of ourselves and inviting them into the present gives us the power to determine where we go from here.

CHAPTER 4

GATHERING PIECES OF LIGHT

Some scenes from life are frozen into place. They stay there undisturbed, their significance unappreciated. Then life unfolds and a play button is hit. The past events are played again in minute detail, and what once seemed just a moment in time is recognized as a building block, a significant turning point, a foundation on which to build so much of the good to come.

The healing connection with my five-year-old self unlocked more scenes from my childhood. As I accepted the reality of the dark events in my life—the pain they caused and the crippling effects they were having on my present—a more vibrant light appeared. The lost parts of my past came into clearer focus and an old hunger woke up inside me. It was more than the hunger for food that I often experienced as a child. It was a hunger for light, hope, and freedom. It was a hunger that gnawed at me persistently through my life, but now it turned into a ravenous need. I searched for the good things in my past, the threads of hope for a happy life that I clung to as a child, looking for their strengthening effects.

Journaling about the past and searching to heal the wounded parts of me took on new meaning. It became more

> *As I accepted the reality of the dark events in my life—the pain they caused and the crippling effects they were having on my present—a more vibrant light appeared.*

than just getting through the healing. It became a place to see the good woven throughout my life, and recapturing those moments was a big part of moving forward. Acknowledging the dark made it more possible to absorb the joy in the "normal" parts of my childhood. I craved that joy and happiness.

Along with the pain and darkness in the memories were small kindnesses, acts of service, and other light-filled gifts. These pieces were never really missing, but the amount of light they carried had been muted by the hidden dark. While the dark things became clearer, the brighter pieces of my childhood transformed into beacons of hope. Images I had always remembered came back to the surface, filling my soul with new strength and power. These visions of hope formed a foundation of light I could build on.

On a quiet Saturday afternoon—Eric had taken the kids to play basketball—I picked up my pen and notebook and wrote down the details of happy memories that had worked their way forward. The bond with my five-year-old self colored the images with more detail and light.

The first day of school came and I still couldn't really say my S's, but I tried to talk so quietly that no one could tell. Mom made me wear a gray plaid dress. "We can at least try to make you *look* smart."

I would have rather worn the one with pink and blue butterflies.

"Just keep your mouth shut." Mom said, pulling my mousy hair into two ponytails. "You don't want to let them see how stupid you are."

Mom put on her sneakers and we silently walked across the street, around the hill, and to the school. The playground was empty. The swing sets called to me as I reluctantly followed Mom to the red brick building at the far corner of the playground. We entered the metal front doors. Voices and footsteps echoed down the long hallway; teachers stood by the classroom doorways, greeting parents and directing children to seats inside their classrooms. I looked at the floor, hoping no one could see me. Mom grabbed my hand, pulled me closer, and stopped. Goosebumps tingled up my arms and my insides twisted into knots.

A kind voice interrupted my worrying. "Welcome. I'm Mrs. Grocer."

I looked up. Mrs. Grocer was young, like Mom, and medium-sized, but there was something light about her—like the pretty porcelain dolls I admired in store windows. She didn't seem scary at all.

Mom leaned down and hugged me good-bye. I stiffened at the unfamiliar hold. She quickly said her good-byes to my new teacher and then was gone. I stood there, frozen, just inside the doorway. Mrs. Grocer kneeled in front of me and asked if I'd like to come in while I struggled to find words that just wouldn't come.

"Well, I am happy to have you here, Tammy." I still remember her smile and the calming effect of her soft voice as she led me to my seat.

Children filtered in. Mrs. Grocer greeted each one and showed them to their desk. When everyone was seated, she brought in a pot of flowers with vibrant gold petals trimmed in a deep orangey-red. Then she showed us a single rose. The leaves were larger and deeper green. All the flowers came from her garden, and her eyes danced with light as she told us about watering and caring for them and how she loved watching them grow.

She read us colorful books, her voice swelling with excitement during the adventurous parts or softening when a character was sad or not feeling well. "Rest time" was also part of the kindergarten day. We folded our arms and rested our heads on our desks while Mrs. Grocer hummed quietly at her desk. Her world was a lovely one.

Writing about Mrs. Grocer and school turned my thoughts back to home. At home, I mostly tried to stay outside, singing to myself and dancing on the sidewalk. Mom worked a swing shift on an assembly line, so Leah was left in charge in the afternoons. She was a bossy seven-year-old and loved telling us what to do.

Even though she was only a year older than me, I saw her as an adult and never thought to rebel against her.

Leah cooked macaroni and cheese for dinner and Dad called her his princess. Once a week, she went to Dad's special meetings with him. She never talked about what they did there, but was always quieter and moody the next day. Thoughts of the old, abandoned house crept into my thoughts.

Sadie and I did not get much attention from Dad unless it was our turn to help with his baths and having "special time." The nights when it would be my turn, I pretended to be far away, dancing or playing in one of Mrs. Grocer's books. It just seemed better that way.

First grade came with the news that Mrs. Grocer was moving up with our entire class. Having her there calmed the storm in my stomach, and I looked forward to being back in her world. Just a few days into the new school year, Mrs. Grocer announced that we were all going to start on a wonderful adventure.

"How many of you like this story we are reading?" Hands eagerly shot up in the air. "And how many of you would like to write your own story some day?"

More hands shot up into the air. I kept my hands on my desk. Mrs. Grocer pointed to the big block letters that framed our large crayon-art covered bulletin board. She carefully made the letter A on the chalkboard. "Now it's your turn. Each of you take your writing tablet out of your desk, and see if you can write the letter A."

The pencil quivered in my hand while my stomach tangled in a million knots. There was no way my fingers would be able to make anything but ugly scribbles. Mrs. Grocer must have noticed my pencil not moving on the paper. She came over and quietly pulled up a chair beside my desk and asked if I would like her help. With her hand over mine, she gently guided the pencil and, together, we made an A. Then we made another. When I made the next one on my own, she looked at me and smiled.

"Beautiful!" she said.

She patted my hand, her eyes radiating love and warmth. I wanted every day to be a school day.

Writing about Mrs. Grocer felt good and light, just the pieces I wanted to find—but then more boxes opened, releasing hurricanes of fear. Pictures of Mom and me in the kitchen replaced the ones of Mrs. Grocer. I was sweeping the floor while Mom stood at the sink doing dishes. I rambled carelessly about learning to write and Mrs. Grocer's smile. I wasn't really talking to Mom, but just reliving the excitement.

"Stop!" Mom's voice sliced through my happy ramblings.

I looked up just as she swung a frying pan at me. It caught me full in the face. "That's what I think of your Mrs. Grocer."

My pen stopped as the picture of my young self with a swollen nose and darkened eyes haunted my writing. Even as an adult, I could feel the pain tingling in my face. Taking a deep breath, I continued to write the events that were suddenly clear.

When Dad got home from work and asked what happened, Mom made up a story about me tripping on the curb and hitting the concrete with my face. She said that I was not only clumsy, but so stupid I didn't think to put my hands in front of me when I fell. I knew that was the story I needed to tell if people asked what happened. This was not the first time I had to memorize a story to hide what was really happening at home. It was not hard to lie—I'd rather believe in the stories than the truth anyway.

Emotions whirred through me. Silently, I closed the notebook and drifted into restless sleep. Heavy darkness pulled me down into the same pit I struggled against as a child, but my fall was slowed by strong and loving arms.

The darkness lightened to gray, then a soft gold. Again, I was a little girl on the familiar path with blossoms all around me. I ran down the grassy hill to the Garden. The colors danced and the trees whispered sweet secrets as I made my way to visit my Gardener. My heart beat happier. New light pushed the fear aside as I told my Gardener of Mrs. Grocer and school and fear and the beautiful letter "A." His eyes danced with color as he shared in my excitement. I felt like one of the flowers, with my petals opening to a light-filled center. I breathed in the light and my soul was comforted.

The desire to recapture my life as it happened still burned strong, but fears of the light in my life being swallowed up by the dark taunted me. I prayed to know what the Lord would have me do with the pictures from my past that would not seem to rest. An image came to me of being in a dark closet. The door opened and the light from the outside room flooded in, defying the darkness. When the two were brought together, the light won the space. I determined to record each memory that was placed before me on the path and the details of light and dark continued to come together. The light that joined the memories made it less scary to continue the inner-child work and gave me hope that healing really was possible.

> *An image came to me of being in a dark closet. The door opened and the light from the outside room flooded in, defying the darkness. When the two were brought together, the light won the space.*

Uncovered memories brought a simple truth to light about how Dad operated in the parallel worlds of light and dark. Most of the members of Dad's dark worshiping group joined various churches in the area. Dad called it a magician's trick— keeping people looking at your right hand, so they don't see what your left one is doing. Many in the group called themselves Catholic and Baptist; my parents joined the Church of Jesus Christ of Latter-day Saints. Mom took us to church when our cupboards were bare or when she spent the electric bill money on false eyelashes or a bouffant hairdo. She met with the local leader to get us free food or to ask for help to pay a bill.

At church, there was singing, prayer, people giving gospel-based talks, and then more prayer and singing. The light there filled an empty spot inside me. It got to the point that I didn't mind going without food because it meant that, soon, we could go to church. There was a quietness on those Sundays that halted the hauntings in our home for a while.

Missionaries from the church brought messages about Jesus to our family and helped Leah get ready for baptism. Mom and Dad argued about letting them teach her. Mom thought that turning the missionaries away would keep her from being able to continue to use the church's welfare system. Dad didn't want anyone butting into their business. Mom argued that allowing us to be baptized would help *keep* others from butting into their business—kind of keeping up a front of accepted behavior. Dad finally agreed.

Mom and Dad were nice enough to the missionaries while they were there, but after they left, they made fun of them and their talk about salvation. Mom said if what they said was true, God would not make her live in such a dump while others got beautiful houses and nice cars. Dad just said they didn't know what they were talking about. He called what the missionaries taught "garbage," but agreed to allow them to come by to "keep them out of our business."

The missionaries kept coming over and teaching us. I loved the stories they told of a Father in Heaven who loves every one of us and wants us to be happy. When they talked of Jesus, something deep down inside of me jumped for joy. They explained that, when we are baptized, we become closer to Christ and can have His spirit with us always. "Jesus loves us and wants us to be happy," they said, "and the best way to be happy is to live by the commandments."

They handed my sisters and me each a small picture of Jesus with what they called "The Ten Commandments" on the back. It took me a while to get up the courage, but I finally asked what "commandments" were. Mom forced a laugh and told me not to ask such stupid questions, but the missionaries smiled, and one of them explained that commandments are kind of like rules that our Heavenly Father gave us so we can be safe and happy. I tucked my picture of Jesus under my pillow and wondered if I could be good enough to be safe and happy.

It turned out only Leah could be baptized because I wasn't eight yet. The missionaries told me to be sure to pray and keep learning about Jesus so I would be ready the next year. A year seemed a long time away, but, with Leah's baptism, we got to go to church a little more often and learn songs about Jesus and love and choosing the light.

The lighter memories came to me more clearly and vibrantly, and the once-dormant memories opened with new life. As I wrote, gratitude replaced fear; light infused the gaping holes in my soul.

Welcome images of second grade flooded my memories. Testing put me in the top of the class; relief at being able to do something right freed me from the chains of my shyness. I found a new persona to lose myself in—at least, when I wasn't home. Library days and book fairs sent excitement fluttering through me. School was freedom, and books let me take that freedom wherever I went.

> *As I wrote, gratitude replaced fear; light infused the gaping holes in my soul.*

The holiday seasons of first and second grade came into view. Dormant memories of Santa and Christmas rushed forward. I loved the light and hope of the Christmas season and its music lifted me to a happier place. Eagerly, I continued writing.

⤙ INTO THE LIGHT ⤚

As the dark truths of abuse exploded into my present, my heart became keenly aware of the kindnesses others showed me during the painful parts of my childhood. When I was able to accept the realities of the trauma I experienced, I saw my heart open to the good I was exposed to during the darkest parts of my life.

> **"Sometimes when I consider the tremendous consequences of little things—a chance word, a tap on the shoulder, or wink of an eye—I am tempted to think there are no little things."**
> — *Emily Dickinson*

When we open our hearts, we allow the good pieces of life to settle into the deepest parts of our souls. Owning the light they carry gives us the hope and strength to keep going.

CHAPTER 5

BELIEVING

C hristmas at our house wasn't like the ones you see on TV. No snow covered the ground, and the air outside was heavy and damp. Only a few lights decorated the small cinder block houses on our street. Our gray, unpainted house looked especially bleak in the fog that came and went during the Christmas season.

Dad hated Christmas. He didn't like the decorations, the music, or having to buy gifts. What he didn't like even more was the attention that not celebrating Christmas brought to Leah, Sadie, and me at school, so he reluctantly agreed to the smallest of celebrations.

Pictures of my first-grade classroom came into focus, starting with the shimmering red and green decorations around our chalkboard. The bulletin board showed off our best Christmas artwork. Reindeer with funny eyes and Santas with heads too big for their stick bodies outshined my small, yellow, crayon-drawn star. Our teacher read us books about the holidays, gifts, songs, and joy.

On Christmas Eve, Dad went out with his friends while my sisters and I helped Mom decorate a small, silver aluminum tree. Then we taped three red stockings on the wall next to the TV. Mom placed a stack of Christmas albums on the old record player as she put us to bed and left. The music filled my mind with thoughts of pretty trees and snow. Peace danced into my dreams of "silver bells" and "city sidewalks dressed in holiday style."

Christmas morning, the sun peeked through the tattered shade on the window. I was usually the first one awake, and carefully climbed out of bed so as not to wake my sisters. The tree always looked much the same as it did the night before—just a few small gifts sent from grandparents that were never invited to our house. No smells of a holiday feast filled the air, only the familiar odor of old carpet and stale cigarettes. I ran to the stockings sitting on the floor bulging with oranges, apples, and nuts. Santa didn't forget us.

In second grade, the light-hearted Christmas fun was replaced with a debate about the reality of Santa. One autumn day, the school playground was abuzz with talk of Christmas, presents, and the silly old man in a red suit. Some of the kids didn't believe in Santa Claus anymore, but I loved the idea of a kind old man just wanting to be nice to children everywhere—although the flying reindeer thing did seem a little impossible. I quietly moved back and forth in the swing while I listened to an argument heating up.

Just when it looked a little hopeless for Santa, a confident voice interrupted the blaring debate:

"But there is a Santa Claus," she said.

An air of disbelief stopped the arguing and all eyes turned toward the tall, slender sixth grader with a perfect ponytail. She said something about love and kindness making anything possible. With shoulders squared and head held high, she turned and walked away.

I wanted to believe her words. What if Santa could do anything? I did wonder why some kids got skates and games and puzzles while others only got fruit and nuts in a stocking. Maybe I just needed to be more committed to the whole idea of Santa to really get his attention. I decided to put it to the test and find out for myself. I would ask Santa for a present.

One Saturday morning, I leaned over the back of the couch and gazed out the window as neighborhood kids rode their bikes past my house. They laughed and showed off for each other as they continued down the street on what I imagined to be some exciting adventure. I wondered how it would feel to have the wind blowing through my hair and discovery just around the corner.

Santa crept back into my thoughts. I could ask for a bicycle. *A bicycle.* It seemed outrageous, but on the other hand, if Santa could really make reindeer fly...

For the long weeks until Christmas, I did my best to be good. I learned to walk more quietly through the house and tried hard not to fight with my sisters. I didn't tell anyone of my plan or even that I wanted a bicycle so badly. It felt better to hold dreams close to my heart just in case they did not come true. This time, I figured if no one else knew, the test would be more accurate.

During the Thanksgiving break, we needed food, so Mom took us to church. The teachers there talked a lot about praying and the power of God. That night I prayed that Santa would bring me a bike. I prayed every night, and even prayed to Santa, just to cover my bases. I felt guilty for asking for a special bike, so I said any bike would do, so long as the tires weren't flat.

By December 23rd, doubts flooded my brain. What was I thinking? How could Santa be real? How could he know me when there were thousands of kids in the world? My test became about more than simply gifts; the reality of a Santa Claus opened all sorts of possibilities for good. I really wanted to believe. I *needed* to believe.

My prayer was a little bit different that night. I thought of the mean things I said and the candy bar I stole from the store. I had not been very nice to my sisters, so I asked if Santa would bring them something too. That made me feel a little better as I fell asleep to the music of *The Chipmunk's Christmas Album.*

Christmas Eve day arrived, and the rain fell hard against the windows of our house. My sisters and I tried to pass the time by playing a game, but it ended up with Sadie screaming at Leah. Mom yelled at us all to go to our room. I flopped onto the bed in a somewhat numb state of despair. The day dragged on.

By evening, the rain stopped. I was still in my room, reading a book and trying to forget the whole Santa Claus thing, when the doorbell buzzed. I snuck into the hall (so not to irritate mom) and peeked around the corner. At the front door stood two young men that looked a little like the missionaries that taught

Leah. They were in business-like suits, wearing Santa hats, and announced that they were Santa's helpers. My heart jumped inside my chest. They talked to Mom about Jesus and love and the season. Mom told them we didn't have anything to give and closed the door. My jumping heart fell flat, and I headed back to the bedroom. They didn't look like Santa's helpers anyway. I told myself. Who ever heard of elves that were that tall or wore business suits? Weren't they also supposed to have pointy ears or something?

Halfway down the hall, I heard the doorbell again, and then the same voices. I turned and snuck back into the living room just as Mom reluctantly agreed to let Santa's helpers come in. They brought in several small packages, some candy canes, and a baby doll. My sisters burst past me into the living room, eagerly grabbing the gifts.

The young men stepped back out the door for a moment and then wheeled in two shiny purple Sting-Ray bicycles. Time slowed to a crawl. Leah held onto the bike with the pink flowers on the basket and motioned to me to come get the other one. My feet didn't touch the floor as I floated across the room and ran my fingers across the soft, white, banana-shaped seat. A warm tingle bubbled through me, from the middle of my heart to the top of my head and clear out to my fingertips. Happy tears gave a shiny glow to the smiles on my sisters' faces. In that moment, my view of the world changed. Santa was real, and everything was possible.

Writing down the vivid images that came to mind showed glimpses of light and peace in the unfolding of my childhood. With renewed strength, I continued forward, searching for and owning the light scattered through my memories.

The new year came—and so did the missionaries, to help me get ready for baptism. That memory transformed from a vague picture of light to real-life images in full detail. The missionaries told me again about Heavenly Father's love and that He sent Jesus to earth to bless the people and show us how to live. He was kind and healed the people who could not walk and made the sad ones feel better. He told them to be kind to each other and to believe in God. He was also sent to earth to save people and make it so they could live with their Heavenly Father again.

The stories woke up a happiness in my heart. They told me how Jesus was baptized to show us the way and how the spirit of our Heavenly Father rested on him after His baptism. He

With renewed strength,
I continued forward,
searching for and owning
the light scattered through
my memories.

commanded all of us to be baptized. They said that when we are baptized, we promise to be like Him. After baptism, we are given the Holy Ghost to help us learn to be like our Heavenly Father. I liked the idea of having help in learning to be good.

The missionaries came often to help me learn about Jesus and decide if I wanted to be baptized. They taught us about faith in things we cannot see and that Jesus promised that with faith, we can "move mountains (Matt. 17:20)."

"Real mountains?" I kind of whispered.

They said yes. One of the missionaries explained that, most of the time, we don't need to move real mountains, but there might be something that keeps us from feeling Jesus' and Heavenly Father's love. Those things can be mountains that need to be moved. They reminded me that our Heavenly Father and Jesus love us and want us to be happy, and they want to help. Part of me believed what they taught, but the other part was too scared to even hope for it.

If I could be baptized in secret, with only me and Jesus knowing about it, it would have been an easy decision, but I was afraid of what Dad would do if he found out I actually believed in Jesus.

I asked Mom if I should get baptized or not; that way, it would look like her decision. She said, "Of course, don't be an idiot."

And so, it was decided.

In preparation, I had an interview with one of the men in the leadership of our congregation. He explained to me that baptism was between me, Heavenly Father, and Jesus Christ, and I needed to do it for the right reasons. He asked if I had prayed about my baptism. I hadn't. He invited me to pray about it and assured me that if I was not ready, my baptism could be postponed.

That night, as I lay in bed, I squeezed my eyes shut and tried to talk to God. It came out more like a whirr of emotions, all mixed—scared, happy, hopeful, and worried. I said "Amen," and could have sworn that I heard God say, "I love you."

The day of my baptism came. As I got ready to go, Mom and Dad had a fight because Dad didn't want to go with us. Mom was in a tense, unkind mood, and I was nervous—not because of Mom or Dad, but because being baptized meant being dunked under water. I tried humming and singing quietly to calm myself until Mom told me to shut up.

After changing into white clothes at the church, I was sent to sit in one of the front pews with several other children who were also getting baptized and the men who were to baptize them. Most of the children were baptized by their fathers or grandfathers. I could not bring myself to look at the man sitting next to me. He was grandpa-age and seemed kind enough, but I didn't know him. All I could do was stare at the floor and study his bare feet. His toenails were yellow and ugly—the ugliest toenails I had ever seen. For some reason, the fact that his toenails weren't perfect bothered me. The more I stared at his toenails, the more the reality of trusting this man that I didn't hardly know to dunk me underwater shot jolts of doubt and fear through me.

What if all the good is fake and Mom brought me here to be drowned? My heart pounded and I gasped for air.

Just when I was about to jump up and run out of the room, the man with the ugly toenails reached over and squeezed my hand. There was instant electricity that went through me and the fear left. His touch felt good, and I did not want him to let go. He didn't.

A few minutes later, he led me into the pool of warm, still water called the baptismal font, and steadied my shakiness with his firm hand. He said a prayer, then dunked me under and pulled me up in one swift motion. As he lifted me back out of the waters of baptism, I felt free and light like never before. The second stage of baptism came the next day at church as several men gathered in a circle around me and placed their hands upon my head. One spoke my name, and then, in the name of the Holy Priesthood, told me to receive the Holy Ghost. A rush of warmth went through me. I closed my eyes and thought I saw my Gardener friend smiling at me.

That night I dreamt of walking in my Garden once again. This time, a new light washed over the trees and flowers. My dress was white and the path under my feet was even softer than before. At the crest of a hill on the far end of the path was a white stone pedestal, curious carvings of vines and flowers wrapping around its slender column. At the top, a book lay open, rays of light shooting upwards from its pages.

A whisper in my heart urged me forward. I had to stand on tiptoe to see what was in the book. Pages fluttered forward on their own and the words turned to pictures as stories played in front of me, showing Adam and Eve in a garden and Jesus healing a blind man. Then the pictures were about me, moving from my baptism to my future. My heart beat faster as images of an older me sat at a beautiful piano, playing like Grandma did. Then, I saw myself at college. Piano music swirled softly and the walls around my heart faded into pictures of a smiling family in which I was the mom and wife. Butterflies opened their wings inside me, chasing away the fearful dark. The future looked full of love, light, and happiness. More closed places in my heart started to open.

A whisper in my heart urged me forward.

As I wrote about my baptism and the picture stories in the light-filled book, it was clear that those events released some of the hold my parents had on me—at least to the extent I could separate myself from the fear enough to be more grounded in the present. During those years, I continued to suffer at the hands of my parents, but the pain and anguish was boxed away more quickly once each episode was over.

I thought of Dr. Abbott's explanation that the division came when I was a child and incapable of dealing with the intense pain that confronted me. To survive, my brain devised a way for me to hide it away. Now, survival meant putting it all together. I gathered the pieces, attempting to rebuild my life while struggling with the gaping holes in my foundation.

⤙ INTO THE LIGHT ⤚

The Alcoholics Anonymous Twelve Step program has helped many to overcome addictions and the trauma that brought them there.

The Step 2 tradition states, "Came to believe that a Power greater than ourselves could restore us to sanity." — *The Twelve Steps, Alcoholics Anonymous*

It can be difficult to accept that there is a higher power when enduring perpetual pain. However, when we accept there is more to this life than we know, believing in a power higher than ourselves can free us to gain the strength and peace we need to help navigate the healing journey.

"Now faith is the substance of things hoped for, the evidence of things not seen." — *Hebrews 11:1 (KJV)*

CHAPTER 6

LIGHT AND DARK

Writing about my baptism opened the floodgates to more beautiful memories from my childhood that came in new, vibrant colors and with more details. I wrote about the excitement of trips to southern California to visit Mom's parents. Images of the long drives to my grandfather's beach house on the San Diego coast came in full color. I was a child again, singing in the car to the catchy gospel tune of "Do Lord, oh do Lord, oh do you remember me?"

The song was a relic from Dad's deep south upbringing, and he often showed off his rich baritone voice with the songs of his childhood. While we sang, the muted desert colors gave way to vibrant greens and cool salt air tickled my nostrils. The brilliant white Spanish Mission on the outskirts of San Diego signaled that we would soon be at Grandpa C's Mission Bay beach house.

The long walkway to Grandpa's house was shady and damp with the intoxicating smell of the towering eucalyptus trees lining one side. The ground underneath the trees was covered with ice plants that spilled over onto the stone path. On the other side of the walkway was a tall wooden fence covered in vines, wildflowers growing spontaneously below them.

The house was massive. Rich smells of the wood that covered the walls mixed strangely but delightfully with the sea air. The stone floor felt cool against my bare feet and the two-story tall ceiling gave it the feel of a castle. Grandpa was tall, kind, and had a light in his eyes when he called us his "little sweethearts." Grandpa's wife, Donna, didn't like to be called Grandma, but she was friendly in a distant kind of way.

Grandpa made sure his cook, Maria, gave us plenty to eat. I loved the fresh cantaloupe and homemade Mexican-style biscuits with cinnamon-y honey butter even more than stepping out the back doors to the sand and playing at the ocean's edge. We were safe and cared for in his beach haven.

Mom's mom lived inland a little, but still in a lush, green neighborhood. She was not mean, but she was extremely strict and had headaches a lot. Her husband gave us treats until Grandma put him in his place with the warning that he was going to give us stomachaches and cavities. Grandma's house was perfectly clean and organized. The dishes had to be placed in the cupboard exactly the right way and every knick-knack had its perfect spot. Even the grandchildren had a designated place—downstairs. Large bookcases held books and board games we could use for our entertainment.

Mom was on her best behavior around her parents, putting on the fake-y mask she wore at church. Dad simply stayed silent and read magazines. Both became kind of paper cutouts of themselves and faded into the background when we were with Mom's parents.

Those memories lightened my heart and soothed the aching. I wrote a beautiful letter to my younger self, full of hope and love. Still, the self-meditations that followed took me to a dark bedroom corner of our cinder block house. There, I saw nine-year-old Tammy crouched in a corner, shaking and hanging on tight to a tired-looking teddy bear. She rocked back and forth with her eyes squeezed shut—like she was desperate to shut out the world. The sorrow in that room melted the walls of fear that kept me from her. I wanted her to remember the sunshine of San Diego.

I whispered her name, hoping to get her to come with me out of that sad and painful place. She silently shook her head no. The scene froze. The message was clear: There was no helping her if I was not willing to feel her pain. I couldn't feel her pain if I continued to shut out the haunting memories as I wrote about the good.

Recounting memories of school seemed to be a safe place to restart my journaling; details of third grade began to emerge. Ms. Phillips was a no-nonsense kind of teacher. She was not much taller than me and had short salt-and-pepper hair and glasses that made it hard to see who she really was. She read us books every day without much wonder or excitement, but she gave life to our American history lessons. It was fun recalling dressing up in Native American ceremonial clothing and learning a traditional Apache dance.

There was no helping her if I was not willing to feel her pain.

The dance and chant gave way to a sick, sad feeling as another box opened, releasing images of another day in Ms. Phillip's classroom. The scared, nine-year-old Tammy came to life in those third-grade scenes, filling in the gaps of broken memories.

Towards the end of third grade, I came to school with bruises on my arms. During writing time, I wrote a story about a huge dragon lady that spit fire at the little girls below her. If they weren't careful they'd be burned to a pile of black ashes. Ms. Phillips asked me to stay in for a little bit at recess so she could talk to me.

"Interesting story you wrote, and scary. Where did you get the idea for it?"

I shrugged my shoulders and looked at the floor. A slow minute passed.

"Those bruises on your arm look like they hurt, what happened?"

I was ashamed and embarrassed. I didn't want her to know that the bruises were my fault for not listening to Mom. Afraid that Ms. Phillips wouldn't like me anymore, I lied and told her that I fell off the monkey bars. A troubled look darkened her face, and she sent me off to recess.

That afternoon, Mom was not home even though it was her day off. My sisters and I just figured she was at the craft store like usual. Leah turned on the TV and we settled in for after-school cartoons. Just as Bugs Bunny came on, Mom stormed through the door.

"Guess where I've been." Her voice was cold. "I had a meeting with your teacher, Tammy."

My heart dropped. After a long stare that froze me in place, she turned and called the school.

Leah looked at me wide-eyed and whispered, "What did you do?"

In a controlled tantrum, Mom angrily accused my teacher of bruising my arm. She told the person on the phone that I was scared to death to go back to school and probably wouldn't return for the rest of the school year. She threatened to sue the school and said she'd be writing letters to the school board.

Mom slammed down the phone, "What kind of stories have you been telling your teacher?"

"Nothing." My voice trembled.

"Liar." Mom grabbed my face hard, screaming words that I don't remember.

I held my breath and closed my eyes tight so I couldn't hear or see the hate. She yelled at me to go to my room. I ran down the hall, hid in the closet, and buried my tears in the teddy bear I'd rescued from a bag of a neighbor's give-away stuff. The minutes ticked away.

The closet door slid open, "Come with me."

Mom grabbed my arm and dragged me to the kitchen. An empty frying pan sat over a red-hot burner. Through clenched teeth, she said if I thought she was a fire-breathing dragon mom, she would show me what it was like to have no mom at all. Leah ran to the bedroom with Sadie right behind her.

Mom forced my right hand into the hot frying pan. Pain shot through my fingertips and up to my elbow. "How about that for a fiery dragon lady?"

Muffled in the background of the pain, she said something about no fingerprints and no identity. She grabbed my other hand, put it in the pan, and just as the searing started, I heard a thud. Mom's leg buckled and she screamed, "Who kicked me?"

I fell to the ground just in time to see Sadie running away.

As I wrote about this awful experience, I was nine again and trembled at the deep, dull pain in my fingers. The monstrous side of Mom that I tried desperately to keep hidden away came to life through more ugly images.

I remembered how Mom grabbed me by the wrist and hauled me out to the car, and how we drove down the highway in silence. With my head against the window, I watched the city buildings move into the distance and low-lying cactus and shrubs take over the landscape. We turned onto a dirt road and stopped. Mom pulled me out of the car, mumbling something about me dying alone. I struggled to keep the tears in, unsure if they were more from the pulsating ache of my fingers or the aching in my soul for making Mom so unhappy. I couldn't look up at her. She pushed me into a prickly bush, got in her car, and drove away.

The bristles on the bush tore at my back and head. Untangling myself from the bristles with one hand, I sat down in the dirt behind a big boulder and started to sob. The ache in my hand blurred my thoughts as I wrapped my knees in my arms and rocked back and forth, trying to make all the bad go away. The sound of a big truck coming down the road startled me, and I froze in place until it passed, relieved that no one saw me. It never occurred to me that someone in the truck might have been able to help. With no energy for another thought or tear, I leaned against the boulder and slipped into a restless sleep.

Time crawled. The sun snuck behind a cloud as I half-dozed trying to block out the pain and confusion. The sound of Dad's voice calling my name stirred me. At first, I thought it was a dream, but some desert bug crawling on my leg woke me to reality. I stood up and slowly followed Dad to the car where my mom and sisters were waiting. On the drive home, Mom went on in her fakey voice about how worried she was about me and told Dad I got upset because I grabbed a hot pan without thinking and burned myself. Then I ran away when we were "hunting for arrowheads in the desert." My sisters and I silently looked out the windows. Dad grumbled about having to drive out to the desert without questioning Mom's story, and no one ever told him differently.

I missed a few weeks of school for my fingers to heal and came back just in time for the end of year celebrations. Ms. Phillips was quietly kind to me. On the last day of school, she called me to her desk and surprised me with the book *Black Beauty* as a gift. I didn't want it. I did not want anything to remind me of her or the trouble she caused.

Even in recalling and writing about Mom's tirades, I had a hard time accepting their severity and her responsibility for the pain she caused all of us. An abiding thought tugged at me through the years, that, somehow, if I could have been different, she would be happier. If only I could be a better person.

As I wrote about that place and time, images of a dark ceremony in my childhood home took shape. It was Dad's own version of a baptism to counter my light-filled one at church a year earlier. There was no font and no white jumpsuit, just me, naked, lying on a table, with Mom and Dad standing above me wrapped in black, hooded cloaks.

The words they spoke blurred as they forced me to drink a thick, dark liquid that caught in my throat; my stomach convulsed as it tried to send it back up. Dad pinched my nose, forcing me to swallow, his hand pressed hard against my chest to keep me in place. I didn't struggle against him; I never struggled against him. Things went gray. In the next moment, Mom was wiping my face and Dad was nowhere in sight. She squeezed my face upward till our eyes met. "You're nothing and will always be nothing."

At that point, the memory stopped, while other moments of fear and pain danced all around me. The anguish of my nine-year-old self pounded through my veins.

In a self-meditation, with Eric holding my hand, I went back in time once again to the mulberry tree house. I closed my eyes and was back in that bedroom corner, standing over the hurting child from so many years ago, and wondered how my present life could exist with such pain stowed in the deepest parts of me. At that moment, another eight-year-old me in a white dress with a face full of light joined the scene. The hurting child looked up and took my hand; the girl dressed in white did the same. Time stilled, and the energies of both girls radiated through my hands, traveling to my heart and mind, lifting the darkness. We were one. Peace washed away the old room in the cinder block house and carried me back to the present.

That peace continued during the next few weeks. The rocking of the earth beneath me steadied and the quiet strength within helped me move forward. Two truths lit the path in front of me once again.

First: Light always accompanies dark.
Second: Trusting in the Lord to guide us forward even through the scariest, darkest sections of our life's path brings peace during trials.

Those were lessons that would come to me again and again.

Journaling helped me forward on my path, so I continued to make time for quiet contemplation to gather the pieces of my childhood. Scenes of more childhood time away from home filled my thoughts.

Light always accompanies dark.

In the summer months when we didn't go to California, our family traveled about an hour and a half from our home to the mountain town of Yarnell. Mom's grandparents lived there on a small horse ranch that backed up against hills dotted with cacti. The saguaro gave a majestic and lonely personality to the Arizona countryside and radiated a quiet strength. They reminded me a little of Great-Grandma. Her personality was prickly and kept people from getting too close, but there was something majestic about her. She wasn't tall like the saguaro, but her confidence seemed to add inches to her height and strength to her slight build. Her hair was a medium gray with dark strands woven throughout—the only reminder of her younger days. Her hazel-gray eyes were upstaged by her sharp-bridged nose and red painted lips.

Great-Grandma R liked horses and she liked everything in order. She worked hard and expected everyone around her to do the same. She was in her early seventies but could work circles around people half her age. Things around her went like clockwork. Dinner was always at 5pm, the table set with poured glasses of milk that got warm by the time dinner was on the table. She never stopped working to listen to you, but simply replied with a quick glance at you and a nod of her head.

Mom was especially fakey around Grandpa and Grandma R and they pretty much ignored Dad. Mom and Dad's stays were generally brief and tense—they usually stayed just long enough for a few hellos and left my sisters and me to help around the ranch.

The year I turned ten, it was finally my turn to go by myself. I was feeling pretty grown up and happy to help Grandpa feed the horses and plant dahlia seeds with Grandma in the flower bed. Dad put in for a transfer with his company that year, and that meant a move to New Mexico was coming. This would be my last visit and Grandma and Grandpa R's. The details of that time stayed vivid through the years, and as I wrote them, the significance of what I learned during that time came into focus. That spring would be the last time I saw my great-grandma and grandpa.

One night after dinner, Grandma and I stood at the kitchen sink, washing and drying dishes. She broke her usual silence and asked if Mom was still planning on making us all follow Dad to New Mexico that summer. *Wait, what?* The fact that she was making conversation startled me; the idea that there was a possibility that we wouldn't go didn't quite register.

Grandma answered her own question. "Of course, your mother wouldn't be smart enough to stay behind. She never cared what was best for anyone but her."

"What do you mean?" I asked the question but wasn't sure I wanted to hear any more. Thoughts whirred, trying to find evidence that Mom wasn't that selfish. My stomach tightened.

"We tried to get her away from that man when your sister was a baby." My brain stumbled over the idea. Grandma went on like everything she was saying was common knowledge, "We're the reason your mom and dad ended up in Arizona after your dad got kicked out of the Navy."

Kicked out?

Grandma never looked at me, talking like she wasn't speaking to anyone in particular. "But that man wasn't supposed to be part of the deal. You know, we would have never helped her move to Arizona if we knew *he* was still in the picture. Your mom tried to keep him hidden, but we found him and never gave her a nickel more."

Her words stuck in my head; my brain didn't know what to do with them. Grandma was sure that the reason Mom came back around was in hopes of getting money.

I wrote down all of this and wondered why, of all the memories from that time in my childhood, this is what was foremost in my mind. Then, softer images of that last visit with Great-Grandma came. The daunting cacti softened with colorful blooms and exploring the desert with Grandma brought out another side of her. She smiled more in the spring-time desert and chatted about its beauty.

We hunted for arrowheads and small, rounded obsidian stones Grandma called Apache tears. We sat together on a boulder and she put the Apache tear she just found in my hand. I turned it over and over, rubbing its smoothness with my fingers while she shared the story of a tribe of Apaches attacked by the U.S. Cavalry. The warriors were lost in the battle and the sorrow of their wives was so great that God heard their cries and took the grief away. He turned their tears to stone, so they never had to cry again. Grandma said these tears were left to remind us all that God hears our cries. I loved my Apache tear and kept it hidden with my Jesus picture under my pillow for a long time. Grandma really was like a cactus—once in a while she showed pretty blossoms that added beauty to her stoic and prickly exterior.

As I relived the times with Great-Grandma and Grandpa, a stillness fell over everything, coloring the scenes with safety and peace. I rediscovered a small piece of strength hidden in my tucked-away boxes.

The rest of the memories from that time in my life seemed void of dark images of Dad and almost void of interactions with Mom. Dad had to start his new job months before we were ready to move, so Mom, my sisters, and I lived in an apartment in Phoenix while Dad was away in New Mexico. Mom changed her schedule to work days, and, once school was out, my sisters and I spent our days at the apartment swimming pool. It was a quiet time in my life—a time that was not haunted.

I rediscovered a small piece of strength hidden in my tucked-away boxes.

➤ INTO THE LIGHT ➤

Throughout my remembering, for every traumatic memory, there was a glimpse of light. With every recalling of a light and happy memory, there was a piece of a dark one uncovered. No life is either all good or all bad, and the presence of one does not cancel out the other.

> **"Research shows that hope helps to lessen the impact of trauma, whether from military experiences, sexual assault, or other traumatic events. A 2019 study on survivors of childhood sexual abuse found that hope was associated with post-traumatic growth."** — *The Connection Between Hope and Mental Health, Newport Academy*

To move forward, we must believe that the light is strong enough to get us through the dark—that hope can help us heal from the trauma. Finding the courage to hope for a better tomorrow will help us hang on during the storms and ultimately embrace the beauty we long for.

CHAPTER 7

THE PATH

The cacti blooms died. In early summer, we headed to the higher desert of northern New Mexico to look at houses. I felt hopeful. Dad would be making more money and somehow, in my mind, I thought that meant the end of all our troubles. I guess I expected a magical transformation, that we would all live happily ever after.

One of the houses we looked at fit my fairytale dream. It was all brick with a lush, green lawn and bushes just beginning to bloom. Inside, a cozy fireplace invited you into the open space decorated with big picture windows and rich wood furniture. It was much nicer than the others we looked at, and I could see myself dancing back and forth from one room to another while everyone around me hummed to the music in this magical place.

Dad did not like the "snooty" neighborhood, so he decided on a small, older house on two acres along a lonely highway outside of town. The move itself was uneventful. The little house sat on one side of the two acres; on the other was a one-horse barn, a corral, and old animal pens. A thousand-acre cattle ranch backed up to our property on two sides. Hills, a few juniper trees, and lots and lots of sage brush isolated us from the other houses in the area. Dad liked the fact that we had no neighbors close by.

Shortly after our arrival and while we were still unpacking boxes, a Mrs. Hamblin came to visit and welcome us into the neighborhood. It did not feel like a neighborhood; there were acres between houses, and she lived miles down the road. However, she was kind and came to visit us with cookies. Before she left, Mrs. Hamblin invited my sisters and me to come to a children's midweek church activity called "primary." Without waiting for a response, she told us she would be by Wednesday afternoon to pick us up.

I was nervous about going to a place full of people I did not know with a lady I only just met, but Wednesday came, and so did Mrs. Hamblin. My sisters and I piled into her big, old station wagon already overflowing with five or six of her children. She drove fast down the winding highway with one hand on the steering wheel and the other applying her lipstick, splitting her focus between the road and the rearview mirror. The little ones climbed over the seats—one in the back seat wanted to sit in the front, and two in the middle row of seats wanted to sit in the back.

At primary, the church was full of children laughing and chattering while women smiled in greeting and showed everyone to their seats. Music started the meeting, and one of the women taught us songs about apples, pansies, a giving little stream, and about music brightening the day and lighting the way. "Lift Up Your Voice and Sing" rang through the air, louder and louder each time we repeated the phrase. The energy of the music woke up my heart and shoved my shyness aside. Light exploded everywhere within me and, for a small moment, connected me to the happiness that was all around.

Writing about singing and being ten opened my heart to another part of me I'd lost. It was almost like I was ten again, waiting hopefully for the light of primary to be an omen of what life in New Mexico would look like. The first few months at that new place were quiet, but as I wrote, the memories of the singing, light, and kindness were interrupted by images of a nighttime meeting in the hills on the other side of town. The images melted into a string of events that I did not want to look at, but the desire for healing kept moving me forward. I recorded the fear and devastation welling up inside me.

Images of a frightened me at ten years old came to the forefront, and I knew the trauma had not ended. Dad's new group involved many more people than the old one had, and, like Dad, some of the men brought their whole families. The meetings were held in the open air under the cloak of night. Black robes and the pounding chanting that rang back off the hills filled my mind. As I wrote, I was ten again, exposed to the sick touch of dad's friends. My heart and mind raced to find an escape, but my body was riveted in the moment. The dream of a better life crashed into a million pieces around me.

The pieces of that dream broke into the present with terrifying details. Closing the notebook and hiding it under my bed did not stop the waves of sick emotion. Eric was at work and the children were at school; there was no activity to distract me from the storm of darkness raging inside me. I was discouraged and drained. The healing I thought would happen in a few weeks and a few pages was turning into months and what felt like volumes.

I fell to my knees in prayer, pleading to be rescued from this dark reality. There was no reprieve; just waves of emotion. I wandered through the house, desperate to have something else to focus on, but fearful sorrow drained my energy. I knelt again, crying for help. Instead of a knock on the door by a close friend, the name of a teenage girl I recently served with in church came to mind—Madeline. With it came the thought that I should check on her. Putting her name aside, I pleaded again for rescue. Her name came to me again and again as I continued to pray.

Annoyed that the thought of her was interrupting my prayers, my plea became more

> *How can reaching out to someone else be the answer when I am so empty?*

energized by my concern for my own well-being. *I am weak and lost, I don't have the strength to help anyone else. Help me!* The more energized my prayer, the stronger the impression came to call Madeline and ask how she was doing. *How can reaching out to someone else be the answer when I am so empty?* By early afternoon, the idea to call Madeline was so incessant that I finally decided to act on it.

Secretly, I hoped no one would answer. But she did. "I can't believe you called, I'm going crazy and don't have anyone to talk to. Can I come over?"

Not sure what else to say, I agreed. I hurriedly ran a brush through my hair and washed my face. The house was a mess, so I waited for her on the front porch swing, closed my eyes, and uttered one last prayer for help.

Madeline came, plopped on the swing, and shared her concerns about home life, college, and the future in a string of words that came so fast, I could barely keep up. We visited for nearly an hour; her energy for life lifted me out of my despair. I gave no profound advice: I simply listened and assured her that everything would work out. She left with a smile and a confident plan for moving forward in her life. Clouds lifted and I was back in the peace of the present.

The answer was clear: I didn't need to be rescued. I needed to act—to reach out and do something good that got me out of my own head and back in the here and now. The pain of my childhood would keep me shackled in a prison of the past unless I was willing to take it with me into the present.

That night, with Eric's help, self-meditation took me to the hills of the dark meeting where a frightened ten-year-old me ran to my arms. She melted into my heart and relief washed over me. Images of another ten-year-old me sitting in church lightened my mind. A large lady with an overpowering, operatic voice sang "I know that my Redeemer lives."[2] The message softened her voice and awakened a part of my heart. In that moment, my ten-year-old self also knew that "my Redeemer lives." I left the meditation with a feeling of awe that even with the pain that surrounded my childhood, there was peace and assurance that someone above loved and cared for me. The experience with Madeline reminded me that God was still very aware of me and offering guidance.

The answer to my needy prayer added a new dimension to my healing. There was strength in simply listening to someone in need. It was like coming up for air after being underwater for much too long. During that time, the leader of our local church congregation asked me to teach the women's organization once a month. The subject was *Spiritual Living*. It felt like God was giving me an opportunity to get outside of myself and find healing in serving others, but unlike previous assignments, this one was slow-paced and fit with my lowered energy level.

Preparation for the lessons consisted of studying scriptures related to a specific Christ-taught principle and reading inspiring stories of others who applied that teaching. As much as I enjoyed the peace that came with studying, nerves got the best of me at the thought of getting in front of the women and leading a discussion. Old insecurities raged.

Throughout my life, I felt like an outcast—especially at church. Everyone else seemed put together and happy. The profound light at church kept me coming back, but I longed for the safety of an invisibility cloak so I could soak in the good while my brokenness stayed hidden. I admired so many of the women there—I wanted to be the mother who taught and loved her children and still found time to share her musical talents. I wanted Eric and me to be the couple that was still in love after fifty years of marriage. And I wanted to do it all in a tidy and well-kept home. Fueled by sparks of hope, I did well for a while on this new goal or that, only to get tired or distracted and end up just being "broken me," lonely underneath my cherished cloak.

Still, something burned inside me, longing to be seen. There were times I felt a distinct, peaceful impression to share some of the abuse experiences I was uncovering. Sharing gave permission for others to share. Our classes turned into open conversations about life, pain, happiness, and tears mixed with the strength gained in sharing personal reminders of our Savior's love. The women I had once seen as near perfect became real people with real challenges. I was not alone.

Admittedly, the open sharing of abuse made some women uncomfortable, and some avoided me. I struggled with the rejection, but the freedom from shedding my invisibility cloak awoke a new strength within me. Coming out of hiding opened doors for friendship; giving of myself renewed my soul. Opportunities to help others provided a reprieve from the heaviness of the memories I was constantly uncovering and made it easier to see the light.

Opportunities to help others provided a reprieve from the heaviness of the memories I was constantly uncovering and made it easier to see the light.

Focus on the light lessened the deep, abiding fear that came with the abuse, but did not negate the truth of it all. Instead, the light gave me strength to accept its reality and begin to see myself as a real, if broken, woman—a woman who, more than anything, wanted to be done with the constant barrage of darkness from her childhood. A woman who simply wanted to be whole.

⇌ INTO THE LIGHT ⇌

Abuse of any kind undermines our sense of self-worth and alienates us from society in general. It can seem near impossible to find the energy to reach beyond ourselves or even see beyond the pain we have endured, but reaching out can free us from the prison created by that abuse.

Finding ways to help others gives us the strength to challenge self-defeating thoughts and behaviors that keep us stuck in the past.

CHAPTER 8

FINDING UNDERSTANDING

For the next year, I was on a roller coaster that soared to freedom-filled heights before descending hard and fast into suffocating black holes. It was exhausting, and I wanted off. In an effort to be rid of the garbage once and for all, I chose to be laser-focused in my journaling to uncover the darkness in my past. I completely lost touch with the present while threatening, demon-like images of men in black robes haunted my sleep and darkened my daylight hours. There was no peace in the unveiling.

Exhaustion halted journaling, and sleep filled the pieces of my days when I was alone. In the mornings and evenings, a ghost of myself floated through the necessary routines. My heart tried to shut out Eric and the children—a frightened phantom lashed out at anyone brave enough to try to get through the wall intended to keep the past from poisoning the present. It wasn't working.

Haunting loneliness brought me, once again, to my knees, pleading for reprieve. Slowly, an image from my gospel study came to mind. It was of a beautiful tree with fruit that represented the love of God. The story told of a path leading to the tree with a rod of iron running alongside to guide those who longed to taste that love. Pondering the image, I was carried away by a beautiful visualization of being on that path. Illuminated by an intoxicating light, the tree drew me forward, but the path was not smooth or easy like the one in my Garden dream. This path was rocky, and sometimes its steep heights looked impossible to conquer. The rod was there to steady me during the rough patches. Focusing on the tree helped strengthen my faith that in His time and way, God would put the things in front of me that needed to be dealt with, and my Gardener's hand would be there to lead me through the storms.

New courage softened the walls around my heart and brought me back to the present. I tore up the pages of confused darkness in my journal and started fresh with eyes forward, leaning on my faith in the Lord for direction. Focusing forward helped me reestablish balance between Eric, our children, and the search for healing the hurting parts of me still hidden. The path was still more of a roller coaster ride than a stroll, but I kept my eyes open to the softer vistas because they steadied my fears.

Journaling and peace took me back to recapture the lighter times of my ten-year-old self. Dad bought a couple of horses from an old rancher that lived down the road. Charlie was a well-worn cowboy with graying eyes, a wiry build, and a belt buckle the size of Texas. He talked to us like he talked to the horses—in a kind and matter-of-fact way. He gave us some tips for riding and told us a little about each horse. Leah was a natural and easily handled the horses, just like she had at Great-Grandma and Grandpa's. I was still too chicken to get on, but watched from the sidelines, learning the do's and don'ts of riding and how to care for the big, beautiful animals.

Focusing forward helped me reestablish balance.

Writing about the horses, Charlie, and working with horses relieved some of the tenseness of looking at those years. As I focused forward, more memories opened, with new detail that helped put the pieces together.

Dad's Satan-worshiping group in New Mexico had more freedom because of the involvement of some prominent community members. Everywhere we went in town, there seemed to be friends of my dad who were members of his group. Mom liked the prestige and was more and more involved with the dark ceremonies. I spent most of my hours with Mom and Dad scared. I walked on eggshells around Mom during the days, and nights loomed with threats of ongoing horrors.

The sprawling cattle ranch behind us was a refuge from those fears. Sneaking off by myself, I wandered down the sand wash that wove its way between the hills. Evergreen bushes lined the banks of the wash, their thick medicinal smell filling the air. The scraggly side of a squatty juniper bush became my hiding place from the world. I spent my time there writing stories with happy endings in the empty pages of a school notebook. On Saturdays, my juniper hid me for hours and, happily, no one at home seemed to miss me.

During that time, Mom started taking us to church on Sundays under Dad's direction. It was important to have a front to keep the Satan-worshiping meetings secret. Even under those conditions, going to church helped me to shove the reality of the meetings to the back of my mind. Sometimes the words of those who spoke touched my heart, but mostly it was the music and the smiles that ignited a happy kind of energy inside me.

At home, the horses gave me more excuses to be outside. I took my time when it was my turn to feed them or fill the water troughs. Our family's new interest in horses and the long bus ride to school led Leah to new friends. One invited her to join the local 4-H club, and Sadie and I tagged along. The meeting started with reciting the 4-H pledge:

I pledge my head to clearer thinking,
My heart to greater loyalty,
My hands to larger service,
And my health to better living,
For my club, my community, my country, and my world.[3]

The message of the pledge connected to the dreams in my heart for something better—that I *could* be something better. The club's focus was improvement and growth through teaching us about animals, farming, home skills, and helping others. The leaders encouraged each of us to have an interest in raising a farm animal. If we couldn't raise them on our own property, we could learn by helping someone else. I chose to learn about hogs, because Lindsay and John Paul—the brother and sister that ran the program—were really nice. Leah chose to learn about sheep, and Sadie always wanted to do what Leah did. They were boring animals, if you asked me—the sheep, not my sisters.

At the farm, Lindsay took me to a pen where four pink piglets trotted around, nudging each other with their flat little noses. She leaned over the fence and scooped one of them up in her arms, held it close, and whispered, "hey, baby," as she patted its squirmy body. She handled the baby pig like it was the most precious thing ever. Lindsay told me that the babies liked to be held close, and if you're kind to them, they will calm down. Trying to hold one of the squealing, squirming piglets made me giggle and, after a few tries, the cute little guy snuggled into me.

Afternoons at the farm lightened my whole world. Lindsay taught me how smart the pigs were and how different foods made a difference in how the pigs acted and grew. Her kindness towards me and the animals we cared for lingered with me and made it easier to believe in good.

The time my sisters and I spent with our 4-H friends made Dad and Mom nervous; they did not like us getting too close to others. So, they decided we would raise our own animals. As much as I missed going to the farm, I enjoyed playing with and taking care of my little pigs and watching them grow. When it was time to take them to the county fair, we won red and blue ribbons and the success gave me a little confidence in connecting with and caring for animals.

We had four horses by then, and watching Leah ride reminded me of the freedom I saw children riding their bicycles experiencing when I was younger. My soul yearned for the same freedom. The confidence I gained from Lindsay and raising pigs ignited a desire to be free of the fear that kept me from riding. One day, when I was home alone and there was no one around to ridicule or make fun of me, I decided to tackle my fears.

I went out to the corral and saddled Speck. He was the oldest and most docile horse. I stood next to him for a while, stroking his neck while talking to him. I told Speck how important this was to me and how I just needed him to be good for a little bit. It took a few attempts to figure out how to use my foot in the stirrup to wrangle myself into the saddle. When I was finally on top, butterflies rippled through me. Speck took me around in a circle at his terribly slow, plodding pace, but I felt like I just won the Kentucky Derby. I actually rode a horse, by myself, guiding him where I wanted to go.

One by one, I saddled and rode the other three horses. Chiquita was boring, and Lady was too much of a firecracker. Ole Blue was last. We walked, then cantered around the yard. Her energy connected with mine and there was a serene power in partnering with this magnificent animal. The freedom was bigger than anything I had ever felt before. Confidence energized me. I laid a silent claim to Ole Blue, grooming her almost daily and going along on trail rides with Leah and her horse, Lady.

Dad's confidence was increasing, too. People tended to like my dad. He was good-looking and knew how to change like a chameleon to get close to people. For one set of people, he was open to others' ideas of how to improve his life or even to help those in need. For those he showed tender-hearted tears. In other situations, he was tough and quick to demean others. Dad enjoyed pitting people against each other and especially liked creating an atmosphere of bias or prejudice against minorities. He could appear the most liberal in politics around one group of people and then turn around and be the most extreme bigot around another.

Some of the men in Dad's dark worship group had management ties at his workplace. He talked of promotions at work and in his dark group and had Mom get more involved in the community to help make connections that would help further his plans. Mom took a more active role in Dad's group that used torture and sexual molestation in their quest for some fleeting sense of supremacy. As I wrote, all the ugliness of dark nights and dark robes came to the surface with the sick swaying of men and women chanting their calls for power in unison.

In the center of that ugliness was the torture and dismemberment of my beloved cat, Midnight. Nausea and grief weakened my eleven-year-old body as I hid behind Mom's cloak. Then, in the culmination of the power hunt, I saw my young self, naked, offered as a sexual sacrifice to the leaders of the group.

I continued to write, and the darker and lighter parts of my childhood started to connect, explaining a lot of why I felt the way I did about my parents and even about myself. I was grateful for church, 4-H, rodeos, horses, and pigs to help drown the pain and terror of those meetings, but it started to feel like I had a boiling pot inside of me and the lid was about to blow. Grief emerged as I contemplated the reality of my early life. Working through the grief inched me forward on the path while images of my eleven-year-old self huddled underneath my straggly juniper haunted my dreams.

I struggled to maintain the adult-child separation as self-meditation took me back in time. Pictures of Dad's mom came into focus and I braced myself against the unfolding scenes. The pain surrounding Grandma D was not confined to a small space—like the closet of my little girl—it extended beyond my eleven-year-old self hiding under the juniper. Its tentacles wrapped around my insides, twisted my stomach into knots, and tore open boxes of new images. There was more to this broken part of me that needed healing—more truth to be uncovered.

Working through the grief inched me forward on the path

⤙ INTO THE LIGHT ⤙

Often, we claim responsibility for our abusers' actions because it eases the sense of absolute powerlessness. Believing we are "bad" means we can believe we have the power to be good and stop the abuse. Truly, the only power we have is to accept that our brokenness comes from the abuse, not an innate badness that we must overcome.

> **"When you accept that you were powerless over the past— that you did not do anything wrong, that trauma happened to you—you can become present in your current life. You can free yourself from living in the body memory of the past. You need not live with the constant stress of uncertainty about the future. Accepting powerlessness will help you move from a state of hypervigilance or hyperarousal to a state of presence, where you can be in your current life, existing within your window of tolerance of emotions, thinking and feeling at the same time."** — *Robyn E. Brickel, Brickel & Associates, LLC*

Uncovering and accepting the trauma empowers us, opens doors to self-compassion, and subdues the storms within us so that we can move toward healing.

CHAPTER 9

CHOOSING LIFE

When I was eleven, Dad's mom moved from California to a small apartment thirty minutes away from us. She would have lived with us—she initially demanded to—but my parents got in a screaming argument, with Mom dealing the winning blow: "You don't need her telling you what to do. Be a man and let her know you're in charge."

It was a message she often used to try to keep Dad separated from his mom's influence. Mom did not wear her fake mask around Grandma D and Dad acted like a whipped puppy.

Grandma D's few pieces of furniture fit easily into the apartment, but she complained it was too small. She also complained about how lonely she was and how hard it was to be ignored by her family. Frustrated by Grandma's nightly calls, Dad decided that my sisters and I would take turns staying with Grandma during the upcoming summer break.

The time spent with Grandma was weird. The smell of cigarettes emanated from the walls and left a brownish-gray mist hanging in the air. Grandma's heavy smoking took its toll; her cough was getting worse. She declared herself a Christian Scientist and that meant she wouldn't be seeing any doctors. Mom said the real reason she didn't want to see any doctors was because she was faking it.

Grandma's words and stories came clearly to mind as I wrote. More pieces to the puzzle of the past dropped into place. She often mused about how she used to be beautiful and had a promising career in the opera, but then she fell for my Grandpa with his wavy dark hair and piercing eyes. He turned out to be no good, she'd say. He took her to California, away from her Alabama home, got her pregnant twice, went out for cigarettes one day, and never came home. She talked about how she was stuck with her kids and never got to go anywhere or be anyone. She told me my mom was keeping my dad down, too. He would be master of his group if it weren't for her. Yes, she knew about his Satan-focused quest for power and encouraged it.

One day, Grandma D asked me if I had any dreams for myself. "Yah betta get some dreams for yah-self and get clean away from that Mama of yours."

Her talking bad about Mom twisted my gut, but the idea of having a dream for myself kind of stuck in my head. At Church the next week, an excited eighteen-year-old girl gushed about the fun of going to a college called BYU and how much there was to learn about life and God. *Learning, happiness, fun—maybe that could be my dream.* The thought of going to BYU turned on a light inside me.

Summer came to an end, and Grandma D talked a lot about dying. "My end is comin', and nobody cares."

Guilt bubbled up from my gut and put an exclamation point on the belief that plagued me my entire short life: other people suffer because I'm not good enough. I gave her a tense but tearful hug, "I'm sorry."

Time with Grandma D made me long for San Diego and my other grandparents. The move to New Mexico stopped our visits to California and Grandpa and Donna's beach house. Somewhere in the middle of that longing, we got the news that Donna's cancer came back and she did not have long to live. It was not the kind of San Diego visit I wanted. She laid motionless in her bed and Grandpa just was not himself. Donna died shortly after that.

The beach house they shared was sold and torn down to make room for a new condominium project on Mission Bay. No more playing for hours on the beach; no more looking out over the bay from Donna's room; no more time with Grandpa's kind cook, Maria. Grandpa quit calling; I am not sure where he lived during that time or what he did besides work and golf. A beautiful part of life was torn from us—a happy place lost to the ugly "C word." The dark cloud that followed our move to New Mexico thickened.

Not long after losing Donna, we came home from school to the news that Grandma D was in the hospital. Mom took us to see her. Tubes connected her to beeping machines and her gray face matched the dimmed color of her eyes. She had been diagnosed with lung cancer, and now it had spread over her entire body. There was nothing more they could do. The doctor said he could not keep her in the hospital anymore, but she could not be alone. The nurses trained Mom in giving shots to Grandma to help with the pain. On a gray day somewhere between the colors of fall and the storms of winter, we took Grandma to our house to spend her last days.

The rented hospital bed dwarfed the dark front room of our house. Grandma mostly laid in her bed, staring into space with glazed eyes. Her breath was shallow and sometimes it seemed she was already gone. One evening, when I was alone with her in the house and thought she was asleep, I tiptoed past her bed to go to the kitchen. She made a loud struggle for air and grabbed my arm before I could pass; her fingernails dug holes into my flesh. The look in her eyes was as fierce as her grip. "Don't let them send me to Hell."

Her words haunted me, churning fear in my gut. I had no doubt that Dad and Mom really had that power.

The pictures of Grandma's last days were etched in cold stone. For years, I refused to look at them, keeping them neatly stored in the back of my mind behind the smells of stale coffee and cigarettes. Now, as I wrote the details, the smoke disappeared in the dust of the walls that crashed down around me. Pictures of the days following her death came clear with the same cold stone stillness of the once dormant scenes.

Grandma's death came without tears or words of remorse. Dad simply made a phone call; the coroner came and declared Grandma dead. He gave Dad a permit to transport the body back to the Naval cemetery in California to be buried next to my grandpa. This gave Dad the time he needed to use Grandma's body for a ceremony he thought would bring him even more power.

For Dad, the death of his mother was another step in his own progress. He believed that every soul had power, and if you performed the right ceremony, their power could be yours. Dad thought his mother's death would be the last piece in his quest for a higher position in his group.

The "power of the dead" ceremony involved all of us and was supposed to create a connection between the living and dead. It was about us all being tied together to claim Grandma's power and banish her spirit to some outer realm. It felt like Mom and Dad were sending us all to Hell.

As I journaled this experience, I tried to keep my distance and picture my adult self simply going back to rescue another scared and broken part of me. The words and pictures came freely with the understanding of how Dad's methods worked. I wrote about the physical and emotional pain that were part of the ceremony and how my heart pounded in my chest. The distance between my adult and preteen self collapsed, and old fears of fiery demons waiting to devour my soul flooded my entire being.

I remembered the ceremony: Dad, Mom, Leah, Sadie, and me surrounding my grandmother's body. Each of us dressed in black robes and each of us followed the prescribed chants and made the required painful and trauma-inflicting sacrifices.

At one point, my eleven-year-old body collapsed and was enveloped in darkness. It felt as if the soul of my young self was lifted from that dark place to my light-filled Garden. A familiar voice spoke, "What is happening in the circle is only for a small moment."

Then the same voice asked, "Will you go back?"

Pictures from the book on the pedestal I was shown after my baptism floated around my eleven-year-old self, and for a long moment, she stayed suspended in the light.

"Yes," was the answer spoken by her heart. Light and peace transported her quickly back to her place on earth.

Peace once again permeated my soul and another part of me healed.

I closed my eyes and was there as an adult, where my eleven-year-old self lay lifeless in the aftermath of the terror. Waves of sorrow and relief washed over me—sad for the horrors that that eleven-year-old part of me suffered, but so grateful she didn't have to be there anymore. I reached for her hand, inviting her forward into the safety of my adult present. Her eyes opened and met mine. We were one. Peace once again permeated my soul and another part of me healed.

⇥ INTO THE LIGHT ⇤

Working through the trauma unleashes emotion so intense that it often blinds us to the reality of the relief that lies just beyond the dark—a relief that will come if we simply hang on. Believing that there is something better than the trauma we are experiencing gives us the strength to keep going, working through the storms of pain.

> **"As a catalyst for positive change, hope promotes overall mental health and may help heal specific conditions, including severe mental illness, suicidal ideation, depression, anxiety, and trauma-related disorders."** — *Carlos Laranjeira & Ana Querido, Hope and Optimism as an Opportunity to Improve the "Positive Mental Health" Demand*

Finding hope in the healing process is what propels us forward. Hope is what helps us hang on in the hardest of times. Hope can change our destination.

CHAPTER 10

GLIMPSES OF HOPE

As I put these pieces of my past together, dormant memories came to the surface. One was when Mom insisted we go to a pioneer celebration at church. Dad didn't want to go but finally relented. The insane fight continued on the way there until Mom's hysteria went into overdrive and she tried to jump out of our car as Dad sped down the road. Then, I remembered a time Dad lost his temper, threw some of Mom's knickknacks, and pinned Leah against the wall. I called a friend and told them what happened. When Leah overheard me, she turned white, and took the phone from me and hung up. "Are you crazy? Don't you know what will happen if you tell anyone about Dad?"

For years, I was disconnected from the unsettling things with my parents and treated these events as isolated incidents. As the pieces of my puzzle continued to come together, the seemingly isolated incidents fell into place, and the picture of my childhood made more sense.

After my Grandma D died, Dad got a promotion at work. The thought that maybe his power ceremony worked twisted my gut. Dad went on a spending spree, buying mom the diamond jewelry wedding set he had always promised her, a piano, and a fancy console TV. He was flying high with grand hopes of positions of power in his group.

In his pursuit of more power, Dad started going to church with us. He thought that the main churches of any area held powers for that area and that he could take that power by mimicking the services and rites of that church. He was on an investigative venture to gain the power of the "Mormon" Church. If he could

get close enough to learn about that power, he could use a coun-
terfeit version of it to gain power in his own group. He told of
being an altar boy as a child (at a Catholic church) because his
uncle needed his help getting power for his own dark group.

Dad decided to be nice to the people at church. He welcomed
their visits and turned on the charm. Suddenly, our family got a
lot of attention. It made me uncomfortable. At home, Mom and
Dad made fun of the people who were friendly and helpful, but
Dad's involvement at church fooled the people there—or maybe
they saw past the front and hoped to improve our family life.
Whatever their motivation, I did not like home life converging
with my church escape. I did not like Dad's darkness clouding
the light I felt at Church. The safety of the separateness between
Church and Dad's group disintegrated. I felt sick at home and
at church, alienated and like an outsider everywhere. Church
was no longer the refuge it had once been.

The suffocating aloneness reached through the years as the
blank spots of my childhood continued to be filled with memories of sexual and physical abuse. The continuing onslaught
of childhood scenes played in my head day in and day out,
regardless of whether I was helping a child with homework or
trying to enjoy our time at the lake. It did not look like there
was any end in sight.

Reeling from the onslaught of awful memories, Eric and I
sought counsel from our local church leader. A year had passed
since the first memories surfaced, and I wanted to be done. I
wanted to know how to box it all up neatly, put it away, and get
on with my life. The man was compassionate and agreed that
leaving the past behind was probably the best answer. Then he
offered a prayer for direction. The peace of the Holy Spirit was
strong as he put his hands on my head. The words of the prayer
were not what any of us expected.

I was told that Heavenly Father would continue to guide me,
and that my children would be strengthened through continued,
frequent family activity as we faced the truths set before us. In
closing, I was told that "these things were hidden up for a time

for [my] protection and are coming forward now for [my] progression." The prayer did not contain the instant healing I sought but gave me a quiet assurance that our Heavenly Father was there and orchestrating a way for us to move forward.

And so, I continued to open the boxes of truth placed in front of me, reliving the pain of my childhood and rediscovering the pieces of light scattered throughout. With every ugly memory uncovered, I gained a better understanding of myself. The path to the wholeness I craved was steep. Prayers helped me move forward and opened my heart to the strength buried within me.

> *"These things were hidden up for a time for [my] protection and are coming forward now for [my] progression."*

Letting down the walls around my heart left me vulnerable to more truth. Just when I thought the worst was over, ugly images of more dark meetings flashed through my mind, bringing torrents of emotion with them. Dad thought that the infiltration of church ceremonies would earn him a higher place in the group. It didn't. Dad changed tactics and focused on recruitment. He called it "fishing" and focused on men that would easily succumb to hatred of different races. Once he could get them to go down the path of racially-motivated hate crimes, they would follow more easily down the path into the darkest holes of human nature.

Dad never gained the recognition he was looking for, and he was angry. He threatened to expose some of the group's highest members. Mom feared the repercussions of Dad's threats. They fought more than usual. Mom screamed reminders that Dad had his own secrets that would be uncovered. The group banished Dad, and the mutual threats muted both sides. The initial idea that Dad was separated from the dark group in New Mexico gave me hope as a youth and as an adult looking back at the past. It looked like the end of the ceremonies and trauma was near. Looking forward, I continued to journal the memories that flowed.

Instead of an end to the madness, Dad used his time of banishment from the group to formulate a plan to create his own faction. Mom decided to continue activity at church as a front, reasoning that no one would believe any exposed secrets if they were active in wholesome religious events. She took us to church while continuing to help Dad with his search for power.

Remembering that Dad was going to start his own worship cult brought clouds of darkness over the present. The realization that this was not the end of the traumatic memories sent me into a downward spiral. New images brought forward the Dad of my childhood into my early adulthood, echoing the same threats. The war between darkness and light raged inside me. The darkness around me deepened and choked out the light and hope of the present.

Nights were sleepless, days exhausting. It became more and more difficult to take care of my house and children. Eric took up the slack with business; neither of us knew what to do differently. The weeks went by and despair haunted everything.

One night, the darkness turned into ugly demons threatening to suffocate the life out of me. Prayers for deliverance struggled out from my heart. An exhausted silence quieted the battle and blanketed me with sleep. A peaceful power transported me away from the dark to the center of a light-filled space where thousands of people gathered in excited anticipation of their turn at Earth life. Each was given a mission or purpose for their upcoming adventure and they were blessed with all they needed to succeed in life.

There was a great sense of equality among all those there, even though some missions were about leadership, while others were assigned to tasks that did not command any limelight. It did not matter; everyone knew that all assignments and missions were equal in their importance in bringing about Heavenly Father's plan of happiness for his children.

An unseen force transported me closer to one of the groups, and I had the sense that, before I came to earth, I was part of that group. The mission was a beautiful one—to be sent to family lines that struggled in the dark. The purpose was to bring light to them again for future generations. The plan was to be part of a flood of light that would squelch evil, just as the flood did in Noah's time. Light disintegrated my fears, and, in that moment, I knew I was born to be a part of the light. No evil plans crafted by my parents or anyone else could alter my mission. The choice was mine. Renewed hope lightened my load, and I came away from the dream with new determination to *be* that child of light.

The dream was familiar—like it had comforted me long ago. Reliving the dream renewed my strength as an adult. There was a reprieve from the pain during this time of remembering. After talking to Eric, a new direction opened in front of me. I refocused on the present and made sure to focus on the good and the light in my past and in my current life.

⇒ INTO THE LIGHT ⇒

The most devastating effect of living a childhood of abuse is the sense of absolute powerlessness. I felt that accepting the reality of my powerlessness to stop my parents from hurting me would destroy me—it felt like I would not be able to live through it if I did not have the power to stop it. However, accepting that, in those moments of abuse, my abusers were in control helped me gain the power to make the changes needed in my life. I could more effectively protect myself.

Recognizing that we have the power to choose what we will do with what we have been given changes everything. We do not have to remain victims. We have the power to choose which path our lives will follow.

In *Man's Search for Meaning*, Viktor Frankl shares his experience as a Holocaust survivor and makes this observation: "In the final analysis, it becomes clear that the sort of person the prisoner became was the result of an inner decision, and not the result of [external] influences alone."

Embracing the truth will help us uncover the empowerment and freedom we crave.

CHAPTER 11

CRASHING INTO THE PRESENT

Fresh air and the company of my children seemed the best cure for the darkness that taunted me. Some days, we drove down the street to the park and played tag. We rolled down grassy hills and ran through the sprinklers. The sunshine seemed brighter than usual and woke up a childlike happiness inside me. During those times, the everyday things that I took for granted, like laughter, smiles, dandelion flowers, and ice cream, transformed into miracles of light and love.

One afternoon, I wrote about the good, and then the beautiful became, well, more beautiful, and opened my heart a little more. The urge to find myself again soared. *This is the me I want to be; I want to live in the vibrant colors of life.* I closed my notebook, holding tightly to the rediscovered fragments of light. Maybe the end of all the turmoil and darkness was near.

My days were a mix of light and dark. As I continued writing about horses and 4-H, going to school, and being fourteen years old, it brought about the realization that, for a time, no dark meetings interrupted regular life. Mom and Dad decided we needed to move across the state line to separate from the group that banished them. I was relieved. The summer before my freshman year was filled with horseback riding and rodeos. Leah started treating me like a friend instead of an annoyance. We were even kind of close for a while. She was great on horseback and made friends easily. I wanted to be like her and happily stayed in her shadow.

In the meantime, Mom and Dad prepared for our move. They agreed to buy a house from a friend of a friend just up the highway from us across the border New Mexico shares with Colorado. Mom told her dad we were moving to a nicer place, so he agreed to help pay for it. The move was planned for late in the summer. All that my sisters and I knew of the house was what we overheard Mom tell her parents on the phone. According to her, we were upsizing to a beautiful house that was twice as big, located on land that was twice as green.

Towards the end of summer, without much ceremony, we packed up our things and headed north. The dry sage brush hills gave way to pines and grasses along the steep faces of the hills on either side of the road. At the end of our journey was a wide valley dotted with fields of tall wheat moving gently in the breeze. It was a small farming community set against a mountain background. Only a half-hour away from our old home, it felt like a new world.

Dad drove ahead of us in the moving truck; it slowed, and its blinker flashed a left turn. The car bumped along a short dirt road looking for our beautiful new home. On the left was a small, tired-looking stone house; on the right was a house that looked no bigger than the one we left. Its old wood siding thirsted for a new coat of stain.

For a moment, time froze. I was reluctant to pick up these pieces of the puzzle and place them into the picture of my life.

"This is it," Mom announced as we pulled into the gravel driveway on the right.

My sisters followed Mom and Dad up a creaky flight of faded steps and disappeared through the front door.

For a moment, time froze. I was reluctant to pick up these pieces of the puzzle and place them into the picture of my life. The adult me did not want to follow my parents into that house. A chill crept through the years and stuck in my heart. *Why am I even doing this?*

I closed my journal and spent the next few days gathering the courage to continue forward. I reread the account of my mission dream, my baptism book, and, finally, about the visits with my Gardener. I couldn't see what lay ahead on my path, but I knew that going forward through the mists was the only way to find peace and healing. I needed—maybe even wanted—to walk through the doors of that Colorado house and find the missing pieces of myself. I opened my journal once again, flipped to the next blank page, and wrote.

The Colorado house sat in the middle of five acres. The few outbuildings were falling apart, offering no shelter for the horses from the sun or snow. The outside of the house looked small and the inside felt smaller. Our worn-out couch and chair looked cramped in the small living room. The old coal-burning furnace left a grayish film on the walls. In the kitchen, the two short walls of cabinets interrupted by a sink and fridge barely held the few boxes of dishes and food we brought. The rest of the upstairs consisted of two small bedrooms and a bathroom or two. Mom called the back bedroom the "master" bedroom and claimed it as her's and Dad's. Dad awarded the front bedroom to Sadie. Leah and I were sent down to the basement to claim ours.

Bare wood stairs led down to a concrete floor that radiated the cold of the cement block walls. Long fluorescent bulbs hummed, flicking a muted light. Leah and I walked through the narrow room leading to two partially finished bedrooms behind the stairs. I took the smaller bedroom and still remember the window looking out to a metal half tube that let in a narrow beam of sunlight. It was dingy and cold, but it was my own little space.

Down the highway from our house was a small church framed by blue spruce and pines planted in a neatly manicured lawn. Once a week, they had an activity and discussion night for the youth. The thought of meeting new people sent knives of pain through my stomach, but the urge to get away from Mom and Dad was stronger.

Our first evening there, Leah and I walked into the church as fifteen or so guys and girls looked us over. The girls whispered to each other and kept their distance, while a couple of the guys came and introduced themselves. Soft piano music started the meeting, and the familiar hymns disabled the knives in my stomach.

After a prayer, we split into classes. It did not feel formal like the meetings on Sunday. The teachers were relaxed and listened eagerly as some of the girls talked about school and boys and family vacations. Leah took charge of our introductions, leaving me comfortably in the background. One of the adult leaders, Sister Slade, took charge of the class and taught the lesson. She shared her own struggle with quieting her mind enough to listen to her heart. Sister Slade invited each of us to share what made our lives full and asked if any had the same struggle with listening for the quiet voice of the Holy Spirit. I think that is when I first became aware of the division between my "church" self and the person I was at home. I could not accept the reality of both in the same moment.

Some weeks, at activity night, we were divided by age groups. Sister Wood was my instructor and tried to encourage my participation. When asked a gospel question, I mimicked the answers that others gave, trying to fit in and not draw too much attention. Most of the scripture stories were new to me, and it was embarrassing to be in the dark about the details, but the discussions that centered on Christ resonated with me, and I could picture Him on the Mount of Olives as He taught and served the people. Sitting there in a small classroom, I *almost* felt His love.

The activity nights became a highlight of my week. I remembered the leaders' smiling faces, the laughter and the stories of husbands and work and regular life. The happiness. I liked the happiness. They were kind to my sister and me. They laughed and smiled easily, sharing the joy that comes from living the Gospel. Their words were not what convinced me, though. It was their lives. Even with young children and the extra duties that come with farm life, they were happy and enjoyed the time they spent with us. I liked how the women fed my belief in a fairytale life with their own real, happy families.

As I learned more about the Gospel of Jesus Christ, there came a stronger division inside of me. The part that was gaining light could not look at the part of me that was chained by dark secrets. Until the missing pieces of my childhood came together, the source of the darkness was a mystery, and I could not be truly free from the fear that hung over me until I solved the mystery.

The half-memories I always carried with me were filled in with detail. Dad and Mom occasionally came with us to church on Sundays. Dad did not like the way the lady that led the music sang. Mom said the people were all fake-y. Most of the time it was just my sisters and me—I liked that. I had my own kind of space at church and my own little space at home. The weeks went on, and the lessons on love, Christ, and His Gospel opened the door to the Garden of my childhood dreams. The light there helped calm the threatening fear that hung between my two selves.

> *The part that was gaining light could not look at the part of me that was chained by dark secrets.*

Our family settled into a different kind of life for those first few months. Dad's commute kept him away for long hours during the days and Mom was on muscle relaxers because of pain from ovarian cysts. The house was quiet. Leah and I ventured out on horseback a few times, but the farmland and fences that surrounded us kept us too close to home. Even on foot, every trail led to a dead end.

Fall teased the air with sharp breezes, and school came with them. Sitting in English class, my stomach did its usual grinding flips until a girl came and sat next to me.

"Hi, I'm Ty." She smiled. "I can't believe we are finally in high school. Isn't it great?"

Great? I hadn't thought that much about it.

Ty whispered to me during class, asking about my schedule. All 4'10" of her bubbled over with excitement when we figured out we had several classes together and even the same lunch period. Her attitude was contagious. We walked to our next class together and I found myself slumping over and wishing I could get my lanky 5'5" stick figure self to transform into a cute-sized ball of excitement like my new friend. Ty made friends quickly, and I found myself surrounded by girls who were easy to get along with. Every school day started with my new friends, and lunch never left me lonely. I lived for school and kind of just held my breath at home.

Writing about the memories of school and being fourteen brought threatening pictures of Dad to my mind once again; dark meetings and ceremonies crept into the present. He told me and my sisters it was time for us to pull our weight and help him start a new group. "This time it will be done right."

Dad craved power. He resented others for his own failures. He thought he needed some unseen entity to prove the world wrong—to prove that he was bigger, better, and smarter than everyone else. When he got reprimanded, his response was always, "They'll see who's really in charge. I'll make sure they get theirs."

The sharpness in Dad's cold voice still echoed through the years and made me cringe.

I wrote about Dad's friends from the old group that came to visit our small, unsuspecting farm community. Dad and his friends met together in secret to decide which methods to use to evoke the help of the dark powers in the universe. Dad talked of fishing for men, ruling over them, and how he could use them like puppets. He talked about riches and power and how no one would ever talk down to him again. Mom talked about the huge house she would have and what kind of wardrobe she wanted. Dad believed that, through the dark ceremonies, he could collect the power he needed to be the master of his universe.

Late in October—only a few months after what I thought was our new start—Dad's full-group horrors started again. The ritual activity became more intense, with physical torture mixed in with the sexual molestations, and most of it was done in our home. Mom's skill at giving Grandma pain shots transferred to giving my sisters and me injections of something that made it like you were moving through Jell-O. Memories and images came cloaked in a suffocating fear that if I ever told, no one would believe me, and I would be sent to jail or that the demons my parents planted inside me would eat me alive. Each threat was accentuated with pain and drug-induced images of Hell. My adult brain knew the threats were ridiculous, but the intensity of the pain and fear that permeated the memories made it impossible to ignore. Fear chained me to the past.

Telling pieces of the secrets to Eric and Dr. Abbott helped loosen those chains, but it was not enough. The process of accepting the reality of the extent of my parents' dark worship fueled the firestorm of emotion inside me. As I relived the details of the rituals held in the name of my father's god, I was thrown back to the place where the light and dark in my life clashed with such force that a chasm broke open inside me.

Two separate parts of me came to the surface at once, fighting for control. Both were angry. *Why? Why did God allow this to happen?* Part of me felt I was drowning in a pit of fire and completely alone. That part prayed in anger, yelling at God for not saving us from the horrors of it all. Another part of me cringed at the intensity of the storm, afraid to let it to the surface—afraid it would consume me. This part wanted to run from the dark, scared of the truth and what it would do to my present. I stopped writing and tried to hide away by sleeping during the days until it all passed. It would not pass.

> *My fear of those emotions left me powerless to move forward on any level.*

Walls sprung up around my heart. My fear of those emotions left me powerless to move forward on any level. The intensity built. I tried reassuring myself that everything was okay: *Jesus Christ is in charge; It is all old stuff, just let it go; If I have enough faith the storm inside will dissipate.* Instead, the fire in me heated up, threatening to explode like a volcano.

Over the next few weeks, thoughts of my dad in more recent years came into focus. *Who was he? Did he continue in his old ways? Was there a change of heart?* I remembered the prayer that opened my heart to the missing pieces of my childhood: "Help me to see my dad as you do."

I felt the need to pray for that again. Dad's previous visits to our home played over in my head; an uneasiness in my soul grew. Threatening words, demands for time with my children, and discreet reminders of his power over me came into focus.

Then, early one morning, I remembered Dad taking me away from Eric and the kids on an afternoon drive under the pretense of seeing the sights and spending time with his daughter. It had not been a routine or innocent outing. We drove past the houses and into the sagebrush covered hills on the east side of the valley in silence. He stopped the car on a dusty jeep trail, saying he wanted us to go for a walk.

"I'm concerned that we're drifting apart. You do remember that I am your father, right? And that you owe me everything. Right?" His words screamed at me in my memory as the rest of that walk played out.

I did not respond to his questions, but simply said I thought we should go home and turned back to the car. He attacked me, and I melted into five years old again, powerless and at his mercy.

I was devastated. I wanted the horrors to stay in the distant past. I wanted to believe I had escaped, and healing was only about the younger parts of me. I wanted to believe that as an adult, I was powerful enough to escape further abuse. The wall between my youth and the present completely crumbled.

During my next appointment with Dr. Abbott, the struggle inside made it impossible to get the rest of the secrets out of my head and into the open. My insides twisted in pain. Dr. Abbott asked me to tell him what was happening, but there were no words—only screaming storms of emotion. I grabbed a pillow off the couch, squeezed it to my belly and started punching. *Just make it go away!* The firestorm raged. Minutes felt like hours; hot tears struggled to fall. While Eric tried to fill Dr. Abbott in on the little bits he was aware of, the two parts of me screamed at each other in my head.

The appointment ended. Dr. Abbott suggested I find a safe, physical outlet for the negative energy I was feeling. By the time we were driving away, I told Eric I could not stand it anymore. Clenching my fists, I pounded my thighs, trying desperately to hold back the hurricane inside.

We drove out to the hills, away from houses and civilization to a place where my screams could be heard by the heavens, but not by the world. I got out of the van and paced. My stomach knotted.

Eric leaned against the van. "Talk, Tammy. What's going on inside?"

Pacing and kicking rocks, "I *hate* this!" hissed through my clenched teeth.

Eric got a cardboard box out of the back of our van and put it on the ground in front of me. "Try kicking this."

I kept pacing. Pictures of Mom and Dad swirled in front of me. The volcano inside me exploded into a full force kick, sending the box tumbling over the rocks. Screams shattered the still evening air; my heart pounded in my chest. The blockades crumbled and suddenly I was fourteen again, bolting towards the box with unrestrained anger. With every kick, Dad and Mom's faces glared at me in the freeze-frame that haunted me all my life.

"Stop it! How could you be so stupid? You are both just stupid idiots. Stupid, stupid, stupid!"

More kicks sent the box flying with me chasing after it while I screamed, "I hate you! You could have had light, but just wanted stupid dark!"

Another kick, the power of my voice tore at my throat. "The stupidest people in the world! Dark does not make you happy; you are as miserable as you ever were. Why do you have to be so stupid? *Stupid!*"

Kick. "Stupid!" kick, kick, "Stupid!"

I jumped on the box and smashed it to pieces, shaking my fists at the heavens.

Somewhere in the distance, Eric softly said my name, and I was back in the present—in the hills with my husband, instead of in the darkness of the house I lived in as a teenager. Exhausted, I collapsed to the ground and cried.

Again, the message resonated through my soul: *It's real. Mom and Dad did those horrible things to me. It's all real.* Eric was angry that the abuse had continued. "You need to do more than just write and talk about it. If your Dad is still abusing and victimizing you and others, we must do something. He needs to be stopped."

It had not occurred to me that I could do something to stop him, but it made sense to try.

Eric knew a detective with the local sheriff's department and called to ask his advice. The next day, we were sitting in the office of an investigator; I told my story. He took notes, asked questions, and, as we talked, though the firestorm smoldered inside me, I felt relief. I was telling Dad's secrets to the very people he said would arrest me because they would see the awful person I was. Instead, the investigator was supportive and knowledgeable. He said the statute of limitations on the abuse of my childhood and youth had run out, and it was in a different jurisdiction. There was nothing he could do about that, but the more recent attack was something that could be prosecuted, if we wanted. I was not sure what I wanted to do, but as we left his office, new light burst through the barriers in my soul.

No more fighting the truth.

⇥ INTO THE LIGHT ⇥

If we don't accept and process the truth of our trauma, it will continue to poison our life. Many well-intended friends advised me not to "worry" about the past, suggesting that ignoring it would make it go away. What I found was that as long as I was willing to keep my parents' secrets, I was shackled by them.

> **"Unhealed attachment trauma can have devastating effects on the overall quality of a person's life, including their ability to be present in their relationships, and the choices they make for themselves. Recovery from trauma is different for everyone. It is important to recognize whether you have experienced childhood developmental trauma and to reach a place of self-awareness with its effects on your adult relationships. Because the effects of trauma are often pushed away and ignored as too threatening to our ability to function, it's important to recognize if there is a pattern of pushing away, avoiding, or escapism in play. Equally important is to speak to a trauma therapist who can help guide and support you in your healing journey."** — *Understanding PTSD, Psychology Today*

Facing the demons and being willing to trust there is a way through the trauma releases us from our abusers' grasp.

CHAPTER 12

THE WORTH OF A SOUL

The missing pieces of my life continued to come into focus. The more I remembered, the more the "why" haunted me. *I understand why bad things happen in life, but why this bad? If Heavenly Father and Jesus loved me so much, why didn't they rescue me?*

I was angry and disillusioned, but I could not quit praying. I became more honest in my prayers, let Heavenly Father know I was angry, and then I would ask for help. Slowly, the anger was replaced with sadness and more pain that needed to be healed. I immersed myself in the truths found in the scriptures. The half-dormant testimony I had gained as a youth came slowly back to life. I spent more time outdoors; the sunshine strengthened my soul as more memories came.

The light and dark continued to creep forward into the present. Sometimes I laid in my bed journaling while my children laughed and played in the other room. Knowing they needed me to take care of them kept me from falling into the muck of the past and grounded me in the present.

Journaling brought more faded, light-filled memories to the surface. There were teachers scattered all throughout my school years that believed in me, praised my abilities, and fed my hungry soul. Sometime during my early teens, a kind piano teacher praised my abilities and a hidden place in my heart opened up and found its way to the present, bringing a spark of something new and beautiful. In moments of playing the piano when no one else was around, freedom stirred my soul. Singing did the same. My high school choir director promoted me to concert choir and invited me to join an acapella girl's group.

Even as an adult, music connected me to a different version of myself, one that was not shackled by thoughts of not being good enough. It was like music let the real me out. I sang along to the radio and in a church choir. At home, playing simple arrangements of Mozart and Beethoven on the piano opened me to visions of hope in the healing power of the good I was uncovering.

The glimpses of hope struggled against the once-buried demons that clawed their way to the surface, and the emotional roller-coaster I was on zapped my strength. Regular visits with Dr. Abbott helped me to dump the emotion and clear my heart and mind, but I could not keep up my usual pace. The house became "clean enough," my dinner menu got simpler, and we hired a friend to help with the scheduling for our business. I continued to recount the familiar memories of my youth.

The summer after I turned fifteen, Sister Slade arranged for me to have a special blessing from a church leader. Excited and intrigued by the lessons about discovering Heavenly Father's plan for my life, I accepted the invitation. On a warm, clear Sunday afternoon, one of the kind girls from church and her dad picked me up and took me on the thirty-minute drive to the leader's house in Durango.

We drove up to an old, solid house made of brick. The lawn was well-groomed, and there were several large, leafy trees on one side of the walkway that led to the front door. A beautiful evergreen grew on the other side of the lawn with space cleared around its base for a few colorful flowers. My heart and mind were unusually still as I followed the others into the house.

An older man invited us into the front room, which was furnished with stately but welcoming old-style chairs, a matching sofa, and end tables made of rich, dark wood. He visited with us for a while, asking questions about school and friends and other activities. Then he invited the other girl to go with him to an adjoining room. He pointed to the scriptures that lay on one of the tables and invited me to read while I waited. I absently flipped through the pages. Peace settled on me like the soft sunlight.

When it was my turn, the old man led me to another softly lit room with a cushioned, straight-backed chair and asked me to sit. He visited with me a little more, and then asked if I had any questions or concerns. If I had any, I do not think I voiced them. He asked if I believed in God, the Eternal Father, and in His Son, Jesus Christ. In that moment, I realized that I really did believe in Heavenly Father and Jesus.

Then he stood behind me and, putting his hands on my head, called me by name. I closed my eyes as he spoke of Heavenly Father's love and my soul filled with light, like a darkened window had been undraped. It seemed that the hands on my head were no longer those of a stranger, but of a loving Heavenly Father. The words floated in the air like beautiful music and then settled in the deepest part of my heart.

As the words "In the name of Jesus Christ, Amen," were spoken, I opened my tear-filled eyes to the same softly lit room. Long, peaceful moments passed before the old man stood in front of me and offered his hand to help me stand. I felt a little taller and a little stronger as we walked back to the living room to meet the others.

The ride home was pleasant, and time reduced the conversation to a muffled hum. The gift of hope and love I received that day still rings clear in the background of my life.

At fifteen, I believed in that special blessing, but wasn't quite sure what to do with it. Dad laughed at my hope and called me naïve to believe any of it.

Mom's response was simply, "You think you're *so* special."

My newfound hope and strength clashed violently with their scorn.

At church, some of the older girls ridiculed my too-short-by-church-standard dresses and laughed at the questions I asked during group activities. Living the Gospel of Jesus Christ was difficult. I failed more than I succeeded. No matter how I tried, I felt like an outsider excluded from the life of light I so desperately wanted, but the love and hope of that special blessing settled quietly in the protected center of my heart.

I continued to journal about the months following that special blessing, and about Leah becoming pregnant and getting married at seventeen. Her marriage changed the dynamics of our family and, suddenly, there was a new intensity to Dad's focus on me. As I wrote, the details of that time were overtaken by shadows of another part of me who struggled to the surface.

All of sudden, I saw and felt myself come forward on my sixteenth birthday. Visions of the candlelit basement in our home and black robes pounded into my present. It was a ceremony performed by Mom and Dad to dedicate me to their god. I saw myself lying on the familiar, black-clothed table, looking into the fiery eyes of my father. A series of physical tortures and drug-induced hallucinations ended with me blacking out and then waking up in a makeshift coffin, gasping for air.

My pen stopped and my heart raced. I was angry at this journaling process; angry that God didn't stop all this trauma from happening; angry at the truth. Fury pulsed through my veins and I hurled my notebook and pen across the room. The tinkle of the pen against the window betrayed the intensity that sent it there. I paced and tried to push the haunting pictures back into the past where they came from, but there was no stopping that memory from crashing in on me. The utter sense of powerlessness stormed into my adult self, spewing a fear that is all-encompassing and still rears its ugly head, no matter the number of years that have passed.

It was clear that the goal of that birthday ceremony was to traumatize and scare me to the point that I felt powerless. The only way to leave that coffin was as a slave to my parents and their god. At sixteen, doors to a hope-filled future slammed shut and I couldn't go on. That part of me retreated while another Tammy took the stage, unaware of the events that threw me into a fearful pit.

I wrote the things I always remembered about being sixteen. At the end of my sophomore year, terror and powerlessness hung over me like the Grim Reaper's blade. Invisible walls sprung up around me, alienating me from friends and blocking my heart from any peace the Holy Spirit offered. Living the commandments became foreign. Finding motivation for something better in my life left along with the snuffed-out hope. My poor choices reflected the loss. I wandered aimlessly the next few months down what seemed to be a predestined dark path.

My wandering was halted by a call from my church youth leader, Sister Slade. *How did she know to call?* She asked for my help in choreographing a dance that all the girls would perform at an upcoming activity for the whole region. Surprised that she knew I liked to dance, I agreed—and then wished I hadn't. Mom and Dad did not like us having any special attention from the people at church. Fear of what Mom and Dad would do and severe anxiety over sharing my secret love of dance with anyone sent me into a panic. The scheduled meeting with her came and went. I stayed home and figured she wouldn't notice.

But she did. She called and asked if everything was all right. I lied, said I just forgot, and that it was okay for her to go ahead and use someone else. Instead, she reassured me that it was no problem and that she would wait for me. Guilt pushed me out the door, down our dirt road, and to church.

Music echoed in the nearly empty place. I followed its sound to the activity room where Sister Slade toyed with a portable record player and an album of old-timey songs. After playing several pieces, she asked me which one we should use. I shrugged my shoulders. She responded with what she thought was good about each song and then asked me again. Worried I would make the wrong choice, I looked down at my feet and mumbled "I don't know." She talked a little more about the different types of music, and together we settled on a catchy, kind of silly song, "Chattanooga Choo-Choo."

Sister Slade gave me a little bit of a dance lesson, showing me basic steps. "Great! You have a natural rhythm, Tammy."

Her words ignited a light spot in me for a moment; my brain quickly extinguished it. She played the song again and put a few moves together to start the dance.

"What do you think?" she asked.

Honestly, I did not know what to think or what she wanted from me. I nodded in approval. She asked what should come next and my brain kind of froze. I just stared at her.

"Here, do the steps with me a few times." My stomach knotted.

It felt like my feet were made of lead as I did an Eeyore-like mimic of her steps.

She smiled at my hesitancy. "Again."

More steps, more encouragement. Slowly, the heaviness left, and I was lost in the rhythm of my feet gliding across the floor. With each step, my body felt more free.

"Now, let your body tell you what should come next." I moved with more energy, and the knots in my stomach turned into butterflies as ideas flowed naturally from my body.

But Sister Slade's needing me and allowing me to contribute gave me hope in myself and made me feel good about me.

Sister Slade and I met several more times, and I went home those evenings feeling a little lighter, like something good inside me was waking up and coming to the surface. A new me was born, and the hopeless, terrorized part of me was boxed away out of sight.

Off and on during my life, people did nice things for me. Their kindness gave me hope in the world, glimpses of strength, and made me feel good about them. But Sister Slade's needing me and allowing me to contribute gave me hope in *myself* and made me feel good about *me*. At sixteen, a new urge sprung to life. I wanted to break out and find the real me.

Until then, I had just wanted to be Leah. She was tough as nails and in charge. If I wanted to be strong, I thought I needed to follow her lead. Now that she was married, I envied her freedom from Mom and Dad. Then, one day, Mom and I went to visit Leah in her new home. She stood outside her small house with a bottle of beer in her hand and her pregnant belly bulging under her shirt. She looked small and vulnerable. I pictured myself in her shoes and something inside me screamed in panic. My ideas about Leah, strength, and freedom changed. A weird combination of images twisted my insides and for the first time I knew what I did *not* want—Leah's life.

At sixteen, that realization opened doors to dreams I barely had the courage to believe in. School came easily to me and good grades felt like a stamp of approval. I really did want to go to college. Even as a teenager, pictures of Mrs. Grocer, my Gardener, Santa Claus, and bicycles brightened the light in my heart and spilled over into a cautious hope for my future. If I had no control over the present, maybe I could control the future. Ideas of college danced around in my heart. To escape into a different world is what I really wanted.

At thirty-three, I looked around and saw the beginnings of that "different" world. It was hard to gulp down the realities of being sexually and ritualistically abused by my parents. Life was definitely more peaceful without a relationship with them, but could I really move forward and leave the darkness behind? I wanted more than anything to sever myself and my children from the horrors that unfolded on the pages of my journal. I wanted desperately to be someone besides the version of myself that stared back at me from those pages.

I looked back at the memory I reclaimed about the powerful blessing I received at fifteen. I took out a typed copy of the blessing and, with a broken heart, read the promises several times. As I read, my heart opened to messages of hope. I closed my eyes and felt my Heavenly Father's love again. If I was to find my way forward, I had to accept my whole life story—the light and dark that were woven together.

⇥ INTO THE LIGHT ⇤

No life is exclusively evil or exclusively good. Whatever the severity of our trauma, or the toll it takes on our minds and bodies, life has a way of sprinkling light throughout our experiences—pieces of hope and strength—to hold onto as we navigate the darkness of the trauma. As we are willing to face the reality of the damage that the heartache caused (even if it's one small piece at a time), we find life-saving light that keeps the trauma from completely destroying us.

> **"To all who walk the dark path, and to those who walk in the sunshine but hold out a hand in the darkness to travel beside us: Brighter days are coming. Clearer sight will arrive. And you will arrive too. No, it might not be forever. The bright moments might be for a few days at a time, but hold on for those days. Those days are worth the dark."** —*Jenny Lawson, Furiously Happy: A Funny Book About Horrible Things*

Accepting both the trauma and the light enhances our freedom to build a life we can thrive in.

CHAPTER 13

PIECES OF ME

Picturing myself on the path, looking toward the Tree of Life talked of in scriptures, I saw boxes in front of me that still needed to be opened. Journaling brought my life as a teenager in rural Colorado back into focus. I remembered one summer when the sunshine warmed the Colorado days and Grandpa Carl came to visit with his new wife, Dodi. The years since I'd last seen him vanished as our family explored local tourist attractions, ate well, and felt his confidence and "life-is-good" attitude. Dodi's sincere interest in me made it easy to share my ideas of college and my future. She listened, smiled, and, for the first time in a long time, I did not feel alone.

The next school year started shakily. My moodiness and withdrawal at the end of our sophomore year alienated me from my friend, Ty, and the others. Choir became my safe haven—it was easy to get lost in singing. A few weeks into the semester, the choir director advanced me to concert choir. My assigned place on the risers was next to a new girl named Barbra who was eager to make a friend. She was funny and nice, and we quickly hit it off. Recognition from the choir director and my new friend bolstered my confidence.

That school year sped by—immersing myself in school and church kept the horrors at home locked away. In the spring, my friend, Barb, talked me into trying out for a coveted place in the pop choir for our senior year. Barbra's excitement added fire to my love of singing and somehow, despite my nerves and the competition, Barb and I both made it into the sixteen-member choir. It felt like the whole world had shifted in my favor. Confidence replaced fear, and for a brief moment, I felt in charge of my own destiny.

At home, I kept the news to myself. I sang more than usual and tried to keep my excitement inside the walls of my bedroom. Life was coming together for me while things unraveled for Dad. The people in Colorado were not as receptive to Dad's religious group as he hoped, and he was receiving some unwanted attention. Mom and Dad also struggled financially. There were problems at work, and Dad's position was being dissolved. He applied for a few other positions in the company and was finally accepted at a power plant in a tiny town in northern Arizona.

> *Confidence replaced fear, and for a brief moment, I felt in charge of my own destiny.*

The world shifted back, threatening to steal my newfound confidence. Barb and I came up with a plan for me to stay with her family for my senior year. I told Dad my plan, spinning it so it sounded like the only reason I needed to stay was simply because the choir needed me. He chuckled.

The next day, Dad was home before me, sitting in his chair staring at the latest *Sailing World*. His lips were tight, and his eyes fixed on the page. "You might want to go check on your mom. Looks like she heard about you wanting to stay here." He motioned to the bedroom.

Mom was lying face down on her bed with one leg hanging over the side. It looked like she just landed there unexpectedly. I tried to roll her all the way onto the bed, but her over-relaxed body was too heavy. Nudging her and calling her name did nothing to move her. A prescription pill bottle lay on its side on the nightstand, empty. I went to the bathroom to get a cold rag to put on her face and see if that would help wake her up.

This was not the first time she overdosed on pain pills. She seemed to know how many to take to cause a scare without getting too close to death. She woke up asking if any of us called "Daddy." In the past, Grandpa sent money to help us out of whatever hole Mom and Dad dug us into. Mom would get better, and life moved forward as usual. This time Dad said he'd make the call when he was good and ready. "This is your mess, Tammy, you need to clean it up."

My stomach was sick with the thought that I was the cause of Mom taking those pills. What if she really meant to die?

I stayed away from her the rest of that night but guilt kept me home from school the next day. I snuck into her room to see if she was okay. She was still dressed in the same clothes as the day before and moaning that life was unfair. She asked how I could even think of leaving her to deal with Dad on her own. "You are selfish. Look what you made me do. It's always all about Tammy."

Usually, I would try to comfort her, but this time was different. Somehow, the guilt turned to anger and then to action.

A surge of strength shot through me, and instead of consoling Mom, I sat down on the bed next to her and said we should do something about it. We should leave. It had never occurred to me before that we could. My mind was on fire with ideas that flowed out of my mouth faster than the usual fear barricades could stop them.

"We don't have to stay here, we can run away to Grandpa's house—just pack up, get in the car, and drive while Dad is at work tomorrow. We will be safe in San Diego before Dad even figures out we left." Grandpa never liked Dad—I was sure he would protect us. "I can start packing and tell Sadie to do the same."

Mom grabbed my face and, with fingernails digging into my cheeks, pulled me in till our noses almost touched. A long moment passed. Her cold stare froze my plan, my courage, and my hope in the heavy silence around us.

Then through clenched teeth, she whispered, "You will never get away."

She shoved me away from her, all signs of self-pity evaporated. She screamed and yelled obscenities about me and my ungratefulness. "If you think you can run away, you have another think coming."

I froze in place. She swished her arm across the dresser, sending papers, books, and dirty dishes flying across the room. A glass shattered against the wall and she swung her hand hard across my face.

"I hate you," she seethed. In my mind, I shouted back that she was just a coward, but the words never made it out of my mouth.

The memory of Mom's attempted suicide and confronting her was always with me and hung in the murky backroads of my mind, long since dormant. Now, new memories flooded my brain, sending waves of panic that ate at my insides. Images of Mom hitting me, burning me, and the fiery hate in her eyes flooded my mind. Over and over, her voice echoed through the years, telling me how unlovable, ugly, and stupid I was. Dad was nowhere to be seen or heard in any of those memories. He did not coerce or prompt Mom to do those things.

Reality sent panic like a lightning bolt from the past to the present, stabbing through the deceit and façade surrounding my Mom. A façade I clung to desperately. Somehow, I clung to the hope that, really, Mom was a victim just like me. In time, she would be free to love me, while Dad would see the good life he was throwing away with his groveling in the dark and join us in a happily-ever-after.

The boxes containing the truths about my mother were more difficult than those about my dad. I never did believe my dad loved me. Leah was his favorite; I was just a distant second he only used for variety. But Mom *had* to love me. *She was my mom.* I held onto that belief like a lifeline that kept me from disappearing into the emptiness of being alone.

The lifeline unraveled in memories of dark ceremonies in the basement of that Colorado house. With every ounce of pain inflicted upon me, Mom's voice taunted and questioned, "Where's your Jesus now?" Dreams of a light-filled life dissipated in the darkness as Mom's words danced around in my head.

It felt like the thirty-something-year-old me was back in that Colorado house—the smell of overflowing garbage and food-crusted dishes clung to those memories. In the dimly lit

living room, I saw two seventeen-year-old me's living vastly different lives. One was forced to live in the dark with the pain of the
harsh truths of my mom and dad. She was cynical; an angry fire
raged within her. The other was detached and alone, grasping
at fading pieces of light.

There was a steep, jagged-walled canyon that divided these
pieces of me. Mists of fear and pain moved between them. Then,
for a brief moment, the mists parted, and they saw each other.
Their two worlds crashed with such force that the reverbera-
tion exploded through the years into the present. Pain axed
through my chest, splitting my reality in two. I was no longer
the regular "Tammy," struggling to deal with the past. The me
I knew was only a small part of a much bigger and convoluted
being. I fought for air.

Pain and fear rumbled to the surface; the whirling scenes
in my head consumed me. One minute I felt like I was eleven,
sitting in a closed room full of color and hope, waiting to be rescued. The next, I was seventeen and anger raged through me; I
wanted to trample anyone who tried to get close; I screamed out
the injustices I suffered and demanded to be in control. Then I
was twenty-something, holding my breath and pacing, looking
at the teenager with a finger to her lips, whispering, "Shhh."

Who am I? thundered in the background of the chaos in
my mind. The eleven-year-old, teenager, and twenty-something
versions of me clamored to the surface, banging on the walls
around my conscious self, begging to be seen and heard.

During my next appointment with Dr. Abbott, I shared about
my identity crisis and the feeling that there was more than one
me inside my head. In the safety of his office, the teenaged
me exploded to the surface with intense fear and rage. She
seemed to have all the reasons there was no hope for me at all
at the ready. In a flash, I became two people. The new part of
me took the stage, and the version of me I was used to stood

silently in the wings, looking on, waiting to see how the scene unfolded.

Dr. Abbott listened and reassured the angry, terrified me that those emotions were understandable. With his acknowledgement that the intense fear and rage were justified, the storm calmed. Just as suddenly as that part of me came to the surface, she retreated, and I was my usual self again. The absolute separateness I felt between those two parts of me stirred a new anxiety. Dr. Abbott helped me redirect my thoughts towards looking forward. The uncovering of the "real me" lay in the path in front of me. Healing would be part of that discovery.

The realization of who Mom truly was and how damaged I was brought the danger my own children had lived in into full focus. Until I started remembering, my parents still had a sick hold over me, and my children were exposed to their abuse and manipulation. My fear and brokenness were ever present in my children's lives. *How many times were they left wanting for my love and acceptance? Was I any better than my own mother?* The thoughts made me sick to my stomach. My heart and body ached to be held in a mother's loving arms. How could I give my children what I did not have?

Eric was processing the same realities—that my parents were still a danger and that they held a sick power over me. Our relationship splintered. The burden for both of us was too heavy. One morning, we argued, and after heated and hurtful words from both of us, Eric yelled that I was a horrible mother. My foundation collapsed.

> *How do I put the pieces back together?*

He left for work. I do not know how I got the kids to school that morning, but I remember their solemn faces. And I remember falling apart. Old sensations of being alone and powerless shrunk my adult self back into a broken child. Wrapping my arms around myself, I rocked and cried in an empty and silent dungeon. *How do I put the pieces back together?* It had been two years since the first memories of childhood trauma. Two years of riding a never-ending roller coaster. I was tired—tired of the ride, tired of the fight for normalcy.

My friend, Kim, came over and found me at home pacing back and forth and muttering, "I don't know what to do," over and over, still rocking in a sea of the jagged pieces that once were me. Eric had called Kim, and in his own broken state, asked her to check in on me.

Dr. Abbott was out of town, so Kim called our doctor who first recommended me to Dr. Abbott. He had me admitted to the Life Stress unit of the local hospital; Kim called Eric to let him know.

The Life-Stress unit experience is eight days jumbled into what turned out to be a pause in life as I knew it. My shoelaces and belt were lost to a bin at the nurses' station, with an assurance that it was for my own safety. What I wanted was to stay in bed and sleep till I woke up from this horrible dream, but they did not allow "cave" therapy. I met with the on-staff psychologist; she was nice enough, but there was no connection between us. I felt like she was just trying to find a quick-fix instead of helping me explore the root causes of my melt-down and what my options for healing were. I left her office deflated.

Daily group therapy sessions and workshops were required, and on that first day, I looked around and wondered if I really belonged there with all those "messed up" people. But maybe I did. I was not okay, what my parents did was not okay, and it was not okay that my children had been hurt. Maybe that was the point—I was finally letting go of the fake, "everything's fine" front and letting myself be broken. It was freeing to admit I didn't know the answers—like waking up from a very long sleep.

That evening, Eric came to visit and sat next to me on the bed. He slid another ring over my wedding band and said, "If I had it to do over again, I would."

Shock melted into relief. Tears flowed and we held each other for a very long time. Setting aside the fear, we determined to face the future together.

The days were long and melted together. The individual therapy sessions were torture—no connection and no reason to feel like I could really open up, but group therapy brought new understanding. It felt safe to share my own bits and pieces in a place where others were open about their traumas and struggles. Trauma was our common ground. Our experiences and pains were different, but somehow the same. We were all broken and looking for healing.

Several days into my stay, we were required to attend a class about how to deal with suicidal thoughts. During the session, others shared their struggle with not wanting to live. I listened uncomfortably at first. Similar despair came to the surface from when I was twelve years old, then fifteen, and then again, at eighteen.

How do I feel now? For the first time in months, I realized that my fight was not to end my life, but to finally *live*—in full motion, with the chains of abuse not only unlocked, but gone. I was not hopeless, just lost.

With my energy slowly returning, I journaled, shared, and listened in group therapy. I searched for the missing pieces that blocked my progress. Nothing came. I read books on overcoming abuse, codependent relationships, and an especially helpful one called *The Knight in Rusty Armor* by Robert Fisher. I could relate to the man who discovered the need for removing his once protective but now debilitating armor.

> *I realized that my fight was not to end my life, but to finally live—in full motion, with the chains of abuse not only unlocked, but gone.*

On day five, we had a group session of a different sort. It started the same as usual—we sat in a circle and shared feelings that haunted us. Then came the twist: role play. The therapist explained that we would play out what taking charge of our powerless-feeling situation looked like. She randomly chose people to play the varying roles.

My turn came, and the therapist had one of the other ladies stand in front of me. She told me to close my eyes and imagine the lady in front of me was my mom. "Now figure out how to get her to go back to her own chair."

At first, it seemed like a silly thing and, without looking up, I told the lady to go back to her chair.

She said, "No."

"Go back to your chair, now." I fixated on the lady's shoes. They were brown, worn, and practical, with laces drawn tight in a neat bow. These were not the kind of shoes Mom would wear.

"I don't want to go back to my chair," the lady in front of me was defiant. "I'm your mom, and you can't tell me what to do."

The brown shoes blurred, and my fingers tightened around the edge of my chair. I took a deep breath. "You need to go back to your chair, *now!*"

My heart pounded in my chest; Mom's hateful eyes filled my mind. I could not look up.

"Go away!" I yelled and then immediately shrunk further into my chair.

The present blurred into the past while Mom still stood in front of me, refusing to leave. Tears burned my eyes; I did not know what to do.

The group leader must have seen my despair and directed the other lady to her chair. "Tammy," the leader's soft voice coaxed me back to the present. "Can you look at me?"

With my chin stuck to my chest, I darted my eyes in her direction and then back to the safety of the floor.

"Take a deep breath and try to relax."

She turned her attention from me and asked what the others noticed about me during the exchange. Then, she asked if anyone had ideas about what could have been done to get my "mom" to go to her own chair. My heart slowed, relieved to have the attention diverted somewhere else. *Am I really this scared of Mom?*

The other voices in the room gradually came into focus, and I could finally pick up my chin and look around at the people in the circle. One said it was weird how I looked like a scared little kid. Another noted that I should have looked up. And then the group leader asked me, "Why didn't you stand up and meet her eye to eye?"

Something in me shifted. "I don't know."

A new light entered my brain, and I felt like a younger part of me suddenly woke up in the present. My heart raced at the idea that I could stand up to my mom and stop the hurt. A dark weight lifted.

Images of Mom played in front of me like an old movie with new color. For the first time, I could see and accept the reality of the abuse she inflicted and her partnering role in my Dad's dark world. I needed to finish processing the pain. I needed to finish writing about the last years at my parents' home. The pain of those years was trapped behind a thick steel door that I wasn't sure I wanted to open. But it was my choice. I could quit or keep struggling to move forward. The idea of quitting evoked the feeling of monstrous demons eager to devour me. So really, there was only one thing to do—unlock that door.

That evening, I wrote in my journal with new energy, recapturing the final year of living in my parents' home. My senior year in high school laid in my memory like a demon eager to prove that there is no god but my father's. We moved from Colorado and I was stuck in a tiny high school with only thirty-five people in my graduating class. Again, I was an outsider and lost. I made a few friends and joined the high school newspaper, grateful to focus on other people's stories and writing about unemotional facts. It was a gray time in my life—I robotically moved through it all, nearly immobilized by pain and despair.

I did a lot of stupid things during that time, some of them under the influence of my parents, and some under the influence of an intense teenage desire to be free from all the restrictions I felt. The internal walls that separated the good from the bad part of my life were cemented by the things that happened between the ages of seventeen and eighteen.

Most of my classmates were talking about college applications. With encouragement from a new boyfriend, I took one more step towards my now almost-dead dream of going to BYU.

I applied half-heartedly, sure that I was about to watch another heartfelt wish get flushed down the toilet.

Spring came, along with my eighteenth birthday. What should have been a symbol of new freedom became another nail in the coffin that seemed destined to trap me forever in the dark. Instead of a birthday party, Dad and Mom planned the ceremony to finish the sealing of my own soul to Satan. It felt like they controlled everything around me. I was terrified.

A fleeting hope that maybe Christ Himself would come down and convince Mom and Dad to change their ways crossed my heart. I wanted to believe that they just didn't understand, that if only they could see Christ for themselves, they would stop all the absurdity. The night of the ceremony, after the tortures I do not want to name, I was forced to bow to my Father's god and, with the ceremonial dagger at my throat, Dad made me vow an oath to give up my soul.

I silently pleaded for help, but no one showed up to save me: not Christ, not an angel, not even a neighbor from down the street. My heart beat hard in my chest. Voices circled around in my head. Hyperventilating, I gasped for air and then everything went black. I awoke sometime later in a fury. Where *was* my God?

That question went around and around in my head. Only one answer came—God did not want me. It felt like that was the end of everything good. Mom and Dad won. I felt sorry for myself and cursed God for my misery. I was angry at my parents and all their stupid friends—and I was angry at God. *Why did He abandon me?* I hated Him for it, and hated myself for hating Him. Rage and the ever-constant fear of Hell churned into an all-consuming vortex, sucked me into a pit of despair and hopelessness. Everything was gone—every hope, dream, or even vague wish disappeared. I wanted to disappear with them.

At thirty-something, sitting on my bed in the Life Stress unit of a hospital, I wrote down the awful details and felt a kinship to my eighteen-year-old self. The emotions from back then mirrored the anguish that had brought me to the Life Stress Center. I did not want to feel it. The next day, my journaling turned again into doodles of flowers and lightning bolts. Sometimes I simply wrote the words "I hate this." In group therapy, I moved around like a ghost in a slow-motion dream state, weaving through still pictures of life in my youth, searching for signs of the real me.

Eric brought the kids to visit. Their faces and hugs pulled at me, and I knew that however hard the road, I needed to get back home. At four o'clock the next morning, I prayed for an open heart and mind and again began to write.

The details of me at eighteen after the horrible ceremony came clearly into focus. In the days following that birthday, resentment towards God and people at church sent me into a tailspin. Mom invited me to join her coven of other women bent on using dark magic to try to force their will on the world. It felt like it was the only way open to me. Despair took me to her meetings, and the horrors made that despair spiral into a devouring pit. More debilitating meetings with Dad left me spent physically, spiritually, and emotionally.

I journaled, and a hopeless scene opened up in front of me. Eighteen-year-old me laid in bed, trembling and exhausted with no more desire to live. Darkness crept in, wrapped its cold fingers around my soul, and spewed it into the hurricane of pain and fear that sucked me downward. My young heart pounded at the threat of Hell, and I struggled to stop my fall, flailing my arms and legs in every direction searching for something—anything—to grab onto. A picture of my Gardener flashed through my mind, and in that moment, a light flickered and stopped the downward spiral.

Sounds of dancing water hushed the whirlwind. The light grew and washed away the darkness while sweet smells of honey blossoms filled the air. Warmth touched my hand, and I was back in my Garden with my Gardener's hand on mine. In front of me was the carved white stone pedestal with the Book of Life that my eight-year-old self saw ten years earlier. Light reached from the book to Heaven and invited me closer. The pages turned, their words flowed into my mind without a sound. Then, with a voice that whispered peace, my Gardener reminded me of the promises I received in the past. Darkness, fear, pain, and sorrow could not take away my future—I could choose whether to embrace the dark or the light. Relief rushed over me with the presence of profound love. It was this Love that made the future possible, and it melted the anger and fear around my heart.

As I wrote, I felt like I was eighteen again, feeling the despair and then the relief of the Garden place—almost as if I was there again. I was not sure if I was in the Garden that morning while I journaled or if my Gardener was there with me, but the promises made to me were as real as the pen in my hand. Gratitude energized me, and in full consciousness I promised my Savior that I would try again. The cement around the walls inside me cracked, letting in a new sliver of light that rested on a strong and familiar conviction that Jesus Christ is my Savior.

> *Darkness, fear, pain, and sorrow could not take away my future—I could choose whether to embrace the dark or the light.*

Eric and the children took me home the next day.

⇥ INTO THE LIGHT ⇤

We do not have to be slaves to our trauma. Being willing to live the life I was given—even with its devastating secrets—freed me to heal and carve out a future I could find joy in.

> "Owning our story can be hard but not nearly as difficult as spending our lives running from it. Embracing our vulnerabilities is risky but not nearly as dangerous as giving up on love and belonging and joy—the experiences that make us the most vulnerable. Only when we are brave enough to explore the darkness will we discover the infinite power of our light." — *Brené Brown*

Today, we can choose which part of our past experiences to build on.

CHAPTER 14

FINDING MYSELF

The two years since these childhood memories exploded into the present felt more like two decades. Eight days of intense emotional work in the Life Stress unit left me exhausted and fragile. For the first few weeks, I went to work with Eric and spent the days in an outdoor lounge chair, resting in the sun, while Eric kept the crews going on a house he was building. I tried going to the grocery store and felt so disconnected from the tangible things around me that it was like walking through a dream. Eye contact with strangers sent the room spinning. There was a weird void between me and the outside world.

Slowly, I came back fully into the present, but nothing looked the same—it was like I was seeing my life with different eyes. There was a gulf between Eric and me and one between me and the children. While the hope I regained in the final days of my stay in the Life Stress unit still burned strong, I was a stranger in my own life.

Eric and I did our best to resume our normal activities. He led us all in fun adventures while I tried to refocus on the daily routines of taking care of the house and children. Eric gently invited me on weekly dates. It was time for us to rebuild our relationship.

Life before all the remembering seemed like a distant dream, and I wondered if I'd ever see "normal" again. The old routines seemed empty. Instead of being on a familiar path, it was like floating on a lifeboat with no oars in a vast ocean. Sometimes, an enchanting island destination peeked over the horizon; sometimes there were only the faces of huge waves threatening to wash me away. "Why?" haunted me. *Why would God let the trauma rip away the "normal" I cherished?*

The question consumed me. It was like I was tied to someone else's oversized anchor, unable to move forward. Every day that I waited for the "why" to be answered, the anchor became heavier, threatening to pull me under.

More prayer. More practice setting aside fear and hopeless thoughts. More practice trusting in my Savior. Picturing life without my Savior by my side dimmed the light I was trying so desperately to build on. I had to believe to survive. Writing helped purge the anxiety, and the effects of the nightmarish realities of abuse were shorter-lived. Still, I was emotionally limited and could feel the energy-zapping destruction of focusing on that "why."

My prayers changed from demands to pleas for direction. My heart opened one small piece at a time and a new question emerged: "What now?" New energy came with the question. *Maybe I do not have to simply hope to someday reach my destination. Maybe I have the oars after all.*

The dark was again infused with light that illuminated the small kindnesses of others and the miracles of hope sprinkled throughout the years. The Lord blessed and preserved my life, and that truth gave me strength and released me from the debilitating anchor. I was finally back on solid ground. I read more books on recovery, pondered what I had learned over the last several years, and prayed earnestly to see my way clearly. Peace returned, but the old "normal" never did.

> *"What is your future-pull—what drives you forward? What do you want?"*

I was still a stranger in my own life and the need to know who I was came to the forefront. Without that knowledge, a clear vision of my current life was muted. Dr. Abbott and I talked again about my identity crisis and how to move forward from this new place. I talked, he listened, and then he asked, "What is your future-pull—what drives you forward? What do you *want?*"

How did I know what I wanted if I wasn't even sure of who I was? The memories of abuse and childhood trauma had shattered the identity I forged as an adult. If childhood had been less painful, would I have felt the need to escape into a life similar to that of the church youth leaders I admired? If I was being true to myself, was being a wife and mother what I really wanted? What was in my heart? If I could have anything, what would it be? Music continued to lift my soul throughout my adult life and connections with positive people was still a staple, but who was I? Did anything really touch my heart anymore?

The questions "Who am I?" and "What do I want?" were tied in a confusion of knots. I knew who I wanted to be—or at least who I used to want to be. It was kind of a potpourri of the qualities in women I admired. I wanted to be organized like this person, adventurous like that one, and kind like another. Thoughts and voices ricocheted between my heart and head.

The three different versions of me struggled again to the surface. The teenager led the way, screaming that I have a choice. She was right, I didn't have to stay on this path. I could walk away from all of it if I wanted. Acknowledging she was right calmed her again while the other two parts of me froze in place, waiting for my decision. Did any part of me really want the life I had? Did I want a husband, children, and part of a home business? Did I believe in the Gospel of Jesus Christ? Heading back to college and a career as a professor of literature floated in my thoughts, followed by my love of music and sharing it through teaching. I couldn't picture either without Eric and the kids. Still, the questions taunted me. *What do I want? What is my future pull?*

For several days, possible answers danced in and out of my thoughts. I pictured myself in a hundred different places trying out different lifestyles, but nothing took center stage. Nothing felt right. Then, one day while doing another load of dishes, exhaustion whispered, *You want joy.* The turmoil inside relaxed.

Joy. For me, joy was different from happiness. Happiness is a fleeting giddiness, like sparklers lit on the 4th of July, but joy finds places in your heart and adds intensity to the light that lives there. Joy is a sustaining power. Circumstances, degrees, and status mean nothing without it.

That light-filled power was what I wanted more than anything. Recognizing the things that brought me joy emerged as the key to discovering my identity.

To muster the courage to open my heart to the joy I longed for, I had to trust that despite the heartache and trial, my loving Savior, Jesus Christ, was in charge; healing and growth could be mine as I leaned on Him. Were Eric and our children sources of joy? Admittedly, I was often overwhelmed in trying to figure out my roles as mother and wife, and it was sometimes physically, emotionally, and mentally exhausting. But how did they affect my heart? When I looked past the exhaustion and self-doubt, Eric was a steady light there. I found strength in having a partner and working together to build a life we loved. My heart was stronger because of our marriage.

I thought of my children. I loved them. In my open-hearted moments, they were a connection to a brighter light than I'd ever known. More than anything, I wanted them to have a better growing up than I had and to hone the tools that would help them build good lives. I wanted them to know love—the kind that lifts and expands the soul. To experience that love, they needed me to be more emotionally present and to be happy. They needed me to *live*.

> *In the darkest abyss, all was not lost.*

Finally, a lighted path opened in front of me. My eyes were opening. It was time for my focus to shift from the realities of the past to the realities of the present. I was living proof that our Savior's love can ultimately deliver us from any web of destruction. In the darkest abyss, all was not lost.

What was my future-pull? To get to a place where I could consistently feel the joy that surrounded me and live with *all* of me in the present. The gulfs between me, Eric, and our children needed to be bridged, and the flickering light inside me fueled the hope that building those bridges was possible.

In the two years of volatile memories, Chance and Lori entered their early teens and the other three were solidly into their grade school years. Getting closer to them started with simply engaging more. Helping with homework, learning to listen better, and having fun together reopened doors, but the road to healing for all of us was going to be long.

It was more difficult to see the way to bridge the gulf between Eric and me. Date nights and family time were the only tools we knew to use to work at rebuilding our relationship. I wondered if his love for me was gone and if he stayed simply out of duty. That belief made it hard to be vulnerable with him. What I did not understand was that he did still love me; he just didn't know what to do either. He was hurting and alone, just like me. We had said a lot of hurtful things to each other, and forgiveness had to be part of that process.

While Eric was figuring out how to move forward on his end, what I saw in front of me on the path were pictures—memories—of Eric and me dating, of our wedding day, the freedom I felt, and then, the births of our children. I collected the light from each one and held it in my heart. Then there were pictures of Eric holding me each time I fell apart. *Who was holding him?* I could almost feel his aloneness on our road to recovery.

I would love to say that in a few short months we figured out all the answers, but the reality is that it was more about making decisions. First was the decision to keep moving forward together. Then, for me, it was the decision to trust in Heavenly Father's plan for us. I needed to take the blinders off and see—really see—my children and Eric and learn to not just hear, but listen to what each of them were saying. In short, I had to get my eyes refocused outside myself.

In the process, I saw that Eric was human, and he needed me as much as I needed him. Learning to accept him being less than perfect allowed me to heal from my own panic-driven need for perfection from myself. I waged a war on the negative thoughts that stirred such havoc in my brain. Action replaced guilt and regret. Instead of writing in my disposable journals, I copied the details of the light-filled moments of my childhood onto the pages of a bound, permanent one—cementing the light into the holes of my foundation.

Harsh self-judgments were my strongest opponents; focusing on "what now" became my greatest ally. Progress was slower than I wanted. Not sliding back into the old patterns was frustrating and difficult, but allowing myself rest and acknowledging my accomplishments (no matter how small) calmed the storms and helped me be more comfortable with being so imperfect. When I relaxed and allowed the peace in my heart to put aside the turmoil in my brain, the light of the smallest blessings gave me strength.

Some days I felt helpless and wanted more than anything for someone to show up at my door with a magic formula to erase the sadness. Instead, God gave me opportunities to help someone else, and He gave me the energy to do it. Thoughts of my church friend, Madeline, and the visit on the front porch swing opened my heart to others. It was not easy, and sometimes I felt whiny about not getting what I thought I needed, but God's way accomplished three things: first, it confirmed to me that I did indeed have something worthwhile to give; second, it kept me from drowning in my fears and doubt; and third, my eyes and heart opened to the times others *did* reach out to me and show kindness.

> *When I relaxed and allowed the peace in my heart to put aside the turmoil in my brain, the light of the smallest blessings gave me strength.*

Little by little, I found the ability to move forward. Months passed, and life fell into a calmer, more even rhythm. Our family looked forward to summer and time at the lake. Eric's love of outdoor activity rekindled a dormant love of nature in myself.

We played and laughed with the kids—it was a healing kind of fun. Gratitude for him and our children opened my heart to growth and change. It also opened doors to finding the things I loved again and rediscovering my love of music, hiking, writing and honestly, my love of personal interaction.

✢ INTO THE LIGHT ✢

For a time, I was caught up in my anger at God for letting so many bad things happen to me. I understood that it is through trials that we learn, but when is enough, enough? "Why?" was at the forefront of every thought and stopped me in my tracks. I could feel myself falling back into the pit of fear and despair. The message of the oft-quoted *Serenity Prayer* took on more meaning:

> **"God, grant me the serenity to accept the things I cannot change, courage to change the things I can, and the wisdom to know the difference."**

When I learned to let go of the "why" and instead asked "what now," the healing path opened up in front of me. In acceptance, the ability to move forward—no matter the path we are on—is ours.

CHAPTER 15

LETTING GO

Days were filled with the triumphs and trials of regular life, but in the still moments before sleep, a deep and looming fear crept its way to the surface. It kept part of me chained to Mom and Dad—a bitter part of me that believed that holding onto fear and anger was a form of protection from any more hurt.

Dad kept me trapped by secrecy. He never even pretended to love me. My chains to him were chains of fear—fear that I would be punished for the things he did. When I told my story to a detective and found support rather than punishment, the chains were loosened. Still, I felt their tug and longed to be free. Prayer kept me facing forward, looking for the answers somewhere on the path in front of me. I continued to journal, trying to sort through my feelings and find freedom.

One day in early May, Eric and I got a call from my brother-in-law. Dad had died. In the few years since we last saw him, he faced a battle with cancer that he ultimately lost. Emotion caused me to collapse on the floor. I leaned against the wall, looking for grief, but in its place was a stunning, quiet relief. The hold Dad had on me loosened and peace silenced half the frightened voices in my head. Stillness. The fight against Dad was finished.

Shortly after the news of Dad's death, Mother's Day—with all its heartache trickery—dragged Mom fully into focus. Eric, the children, and I went to church and listened to songs about gathering blossoms in meadows and love at home. The bench beneath me felt hard and cold. By the time two men finished talking about their wonderful mothers and what a blessing mothers are, I wanted to throw up. Heartache transformed into anger.

The old, familiar chains felt tight on my hands and feet. After all I'd been through, fear of Mom still had me shackled. I was on a huge carousel, thinking the horse I rode would take me into the sunshine, but, instead, time and time again, I ended up in the same ugly spot. I hated Mom and the fear that constantly tried to pull me into that old, familiar, black pit. I hated that I felt so limited in mothering my own children. The hate was poisoning me and transformed into a hurricane of negative energy that threatened to devour the light I craved. Prayer after prayer after prayer banged against the wall of fear, anger, and hurt that kept my heart closed to Heaven. I wanted off the carousel.

At five o'clock one morning, my friend Kim and I met for our routine run to the golf course and back. Stars from the night before sprinkled the skies, and it felt good to take in the still air filled with faint smells of watered grass and sweet blossoms. We walked down the street, stopping at the corner to stretch our legs. Idle chat broke the silence. We picked up the pace, and my body and mind came to life. The rhythmic sound of our feet pounding the pavement echoed the pounding in my heart. My insides felt flipped out of order and I was ashamed of the hate that churned inside me.

"I feel haunted by my mom and just can't seem to shake it."

"What do you mean, haunted?" Kim asked.

She listened intently as I tried to sort out the emotions that kept me trapped. It felt like my words fell onto safe ground—that the stillness of the morning and the kindness of my friend would protect my secrets.

My insides felt flipped out of order and I was ashamed of the hate that churned inside me.

The sun peeked over the mountains and we made the loop, heading up the hill towards home. My accelerating heartbeat freed the dark emotion. The hurt that fueled the anger exploded to the surface with gasping sobs. The wall cracked. I stopped halfway up the hill, trying to catch my breath, not knowing if I could continue. With a gentle nudge to my elbow, Kim encouraged me forward. No more was said as we made our way back to where we started. Kim and I said our goodbyes and in the stillness of the early morning drive, one word came into focus: forgive.

The thought knifed my stomach. It felt like forgiving meant that the soul-ripping Mom had done didn't matter and the emotional crippling that happened at her hand meant nothing. A war raged inside me. Two sides of me fought for control. The one that prayed tried desperately to hang onto hope and find a way to follow the loving teachings of Jesus. She wanted to believe there was a way forward. The one that tried to protect was determined to hang on to the hate and anger. The Protector was sure that the Pray-er would fold without the anger to keep her safe. The Pray-er just wanted to be free from the chains of hate.

All of the sides to me in my head wanted to run away until the fear was gone, but there was nowhere to run to where the battle wouldn't follow. The anger couldn't be talked away and fighting against it only made it bigger. At my next visit with Dr. Abbott, he listened to me rant and cry while I paced back and forth in his office. I needed an outlet for the anger. I really wanted to hit something.

On the way home, I stopped at a sporting goods store and bought a punching bag. Eric hung it in the garage for me, gave me some workout gloves, and then showed me how to hold my wrist straight and drive the punch by turning my body. I taped a scribbled cartoon-like picture of my mom on the front of the bag and started punching. A hurricane of hate and anger fueled every hit, releasing more power than I knew I had. Each punch tore at the picture and ripped apart the barrier between the two versions of me and exposed the lies that bound them.

At the very center of the hurricane was an unspoken conviction that I was tied to Mom with bonds that could never be broken. The very core of my relationship with her was based on the deep belief that I was responsible for her. If she was mean, it was my fault. If she was unhappy, it was my fault. If she took her own life, it would be because I didn't love her well enough.

Underneath the Protector's mask was the seventeen-year-old me that tried to get away, but was shackled by Mom's attempted suicide. For years, that part of me sawed away at the bonds by trying to be perfect enough for Mom to be happy. If Mom was happy, maybe freedom would follow. Forgiving Mom felt like it was more about forgiving myself. Somewhere inside was the twisted belief that I had to forgive myself for her actions. Recognizing what was at the core of the unresolved pain settled the storm and, slowly, the way forward came into view.

I am not responsible for Mom's actions. Accepting and believing that truth was the goal. Unraveling the lies that kept the truth hidden was the way. More journaling exposed Mom's willing involvement in occult activities when I was very young. Memories of home life when Dad was not around crept to the surface, exposing more traumatized parts of me trying to hide in the same dirty closet.

Fear was the bond that tied me to Mom. Fully accepting the trauma and the extent of the pain inflicted by her loosened the hold she had on me and freed the part of me that acted as my Protector to come into the present. *Truth* became my protection.

The storm settled, but the need for answers raged. The old sayings "forgive and forget" and "turn the other cheek" and the command to "honor thy father and thy mother"[4] intensified the clouds of confusion and kept me tied to the carousel. Old ideas of forgiveness swirled in my head. Childhood experience taught that, no matter what pain was inflicted on me, it was my fault. Forgiveness meant acknowledging that the abuser was not to blame. The idea of honoring my parents supported that idea. In my childish mind, "honoring" meant putting someone on a pedestal and only seeing the good. The fact that those assumptions were flawed was easy to accept logically, but the emotional thinking was not so easily discarded.

> *Truth became my protection.*

How did honoring and forgiving my parents factor into the murky path I was on to overcome the pain inflicted by them? Looking around at how the word "honor" was used in the adult world, it often meant "praising" or "worshiping." That type of honoring didn't really go with the messages of the First Commandment given to Moses on Mount Sinai.[5] Honoring our Heavenly Father and our Savior clearly is first and foremost. The only way I could honor both my Heavenly Father and my earthly parents had to do with reinterpreting "honor" to mean simply living the best life I could. That change in perspective lit a spark of understanding within me. Living a life of kindness and love could shed an honorable light on them and the idea of it calmed my soul. Still, the "why" and "how" of forgiveness lurked at the edges of the peace.

In the first months of remembering the abuse, I rushed to forgive, thinking that forgiving my parents would erase all the bad and keep me from having to open more boxes of trauma. The attempt to bury the pain with superficial forgiving unleashed new hurricanes of anger and fear. Holding onto the anger and not being willing to forgive doused the light I so desperately needed. Trying to use forgiveness as an escape only tightened the hold the trauma had on me. Either way, there was no moving forward.

There had to be more to Christ's invitation to forgive. I read whole chapters instead of single verses in the New Testament, searching in Jesus' own words for answers. In the eighteenth chapter in Matthew (before the counsel to forgive "seventy times seven"[6]), Jesus said, "But whoso shall offend one of these little ones which believe in me, it were better for him that a millstone were hanged about his neck, and that he were drowned in the depth of the sea."[7]

Christ's love and care for the little ones comforted my pain and opened my eyes to a clearer picture of forgiveness. In these chapters, Christ gave a fuller view of how we should structure our relationships with others. New messages emerged from my study.

True forgiveness is not okaying the abuse but trusting in the healing power of the Atonement of Jesus Christ. Just as His grace can heal the wounds of my own sins, it can heal the wounds caused by others. Hate, anger, and vengeance are contrary to a forgiving heart, and that is what our Savior wants us to avoid. Forgiveness does not mean a renewed relationship if that relationship can cause harm.

New understanding quieted my mind, but nothing could instantly heal my heart. No matter how much emotional and physical pain she had inflicted, I wanted a mom. I needed a mom that loved me. That need made it harder to let go of the lies woven throughout my childhood—thick, strangling beliefs that the pain inflicted on me was my fault. Guilt spun lies about my own self-worth, my ability to choose for myself, and that, somehow, I was only an appendage of Mom without my own identity. Holding onto the lies shackled me to the pain.

Forgiveness does not mean a renewed relationship if that relationship can cause harm.

I prayed, wrote, and spent time with friends hiking in the mountains, searching for freedom and healing. The parts of me that held the mom-inflicted pain struggled to the surface and scattered pieces of truth on the path in front of me. Through tears and heartache, I gathered the pieces, slowly letting go of the make-believe mom I wanted and finally seeing Mom as the person she really was. Decades of sadness and need exploded into the present and transformed into a child-like poem:

I longed for a Mother's arms to hold and gently care;
To love, protect, and reassure to silence little fears;
To laugh, to play, to hold me when I shed a tear.
I needed a Mother to show the way; to teach and lend a hand;
To shelter, love and simply say, "You can."
To have a Mother's loving touch would truly heal my heart.

The lies began to dissolve and I could see Mom and myself more rationally. Because she never admitted to her part in any of my pain, she was still a danger to my family and to me. I needed closure so I could move on. A eulogy came next.

The Death of a Dream
Today I shed a tear, not for the Mother I had
But the one she could have been.
My heart aches: not for her arms to hold me
But for the arms of one who loves.
I cry for all the things that should have been but never were.
The page has turned:
I wait not for the one who should have loved me
But for the one who will.

On a stormy day, I took the eulogy, the poem, and a single red rose to the local cemetery. Kneeling among the headstones, I read the poems aloud, tore the petals off the flower one by one and watched the wind carry them away. Rain and tears ran down my face and, for a moment, it felt like Heaven cried with me. The chains were dissolving, but they left a tremendous aching in my heart for a mother's love. Referring to Mom by her given name, Edna, helped soften the pain.

Over time, God opened my eyes—and my heart—to women in my life that could soothe the aching. Eric's mom treated me like her own from the time we met. Her confidence and positivity rubbed off on me and her encouragement to me to follow my dreams lifted my vision to better things. A lovely lady a little older than Edna invited me to join her in quilt-making and choir. She shared her own stories and listened to mine. Her kind heart touched my soul, healing some of the brokenness. It turns out that God cannot make the people who should love you, love you, but He can—and will—surround you with people who will.

Gratitude for the mother figures in my life softened the pain of letting go of Edna. The ability to see my relationship with her as it really was improved over time, and clarity severed the bonds of imprisonment one by one. Learning—accepting—that I am not her, and that I am in control of my own being, freed me to explore what I was learning about true forgiveness.

Anger still haunted my attempts to forgive and guilt caused by the anger came with it. I wanted to be released from the weight, but didn't know how. The heaviness exhausted me and drove me to my knees time and time again.

> *It turns out that God cannot make the people who should love you, love you, but He can—and will—surround you with people who will.*

Finally, in the early morning, hours after a sleepless night, I cried my anger to God and admitted the hate in my heart. If He was all-powerful, how could He let my mom torture my soul and smash it and my heart into ruin? Anger pulsed in my veins, screaming to be heard. I ran to the garage to attack the punching bag, and with a hit that sent shockwaves up my arm, I collapsed to the cold concrete floor, wracked with the sobs of exploding hatred. The wall around my heart shattered into a thousand pieces. Vulnerable and exposed, the anger quieted while cold seeped into my bones and woke me to the present. I struggled to my feet, back into the quiet of the sleeping house and back to the comfort of my familiar chair. In the calm, the question of "What now?" emerged with the rising sun.

Tears clouded the path in front of me and silent pleas for help reached out in the hope that someone was listening. Looking back, I could see that even when I strayed or was sucked into dark pits, flickers of light invited me forward. In the background of my life, my Gardener was there, gently lifting and guiding me when the pain clouded my ability to see or feel him.

In that still moment, a soft voice touched my heart. "Heavenly Father weeps over your pain and is angered at the abuse and trauma poured on you and others at the hands of your parents."

Relief that my pain and anger were heard and carried by One much stronger than me lightened my burden. For a brief moment, I could taste the cool, refreshing water my Gardener offered me so many years ago. I didn't need to fix the hate, but allow it to be healed. I *felt* my Heavenly Father's love and validation. Finally, I could lay my anguish, hate, anger, and bitterness at the feet of my loving Savior. I was learning that in every trial, there is strength; in every darkness, there is light. Our Savior, Jesus Christ, finds us in the depths of our anguish, offering His hand to lift us back into the light. His light.

> *My life became my own—my choices, my story. I was learning how to live.*

There was a reprieve from opening boxes, and I could simply enjoy being in the present. Honesty about the trauma and the light that helped me through it filled the empty spaces in my soul with a new kind of freedom. It was a freedom to see myself more clearly—the good, the bad, and the in-between. My life became my own—*my* choices, *my* story. I was learning how to *live*.

⇥ INTO THE LIGHT ⇤

"Forgiveness doesn't mean forgetting or excusing the harm done to you. It also doesn't necessarily mean making up with the person who caused the harm. Forgiveness brings a kind of peace that allows you to focus on yourself and helps you go on with life…

Forgiveness can lead to:

- Healthier relationships
- Improved mental health
- Less anxiety, stress and hostility
- Fewer symptoms of depression
- Lower blood pressure
- A stronger immune system
- Improved heart health
- Improved self-esteem."

— *Forgiveness, Mayo Clinic*

Ultimately, forgiveness is not about the other person, but about giving up burdens so that we can use our strength to move forward. Choosing forgiveness is choosing freedom.

CHAPTER 16

THE TAPESTRY

The other night, thoughts of forgiveness, pain, healing, and fear floated in and around my exhausted mind until my pulse slowed and I slipped into a light-filled dream. The sound of water dancing along a creek bed drew me into a vision of green, rolling hills and the sensation of air thick with the smell of spring. I stood for a moment in the light and peace of my beautiful Garden. In my arms was a gift: a rolled-up tapestry that was as big as a room but as light to carry as a baby blanket. Then, in the soft sunlight, I saw Him—the Gardener of my childhood. His smile woke up the childlike happiness in my heart and carried me to His side.

We sat on the familiar bench next to the singing creek, and, together, we unrolled the gift. It was made up of a million threads in a thousand colors, woven together in a way that moved the fabric to a soulful melody. Dark threads intensified the brightness of the color while a vibrant white radiated warmth in every strand. With my Gardener's hand on mine, I ran my fingers over the fabric, feeling its energy pulse through me. The tapestry was whole. I was whole.

In those quiet moments on the bench with the Gardener, my eyes opened to others gathering around us. Each brought a rich and unique tapestry with them, with colors that joined the music of my own. My heart was full with gratitude for those that had touched my life over the years and whose influence gave me the energy to hold on when I didn't think I could—the energy that led me to this moment.

It has been a long road since I first started writing about the events of my childhood. I have told secrets that I never thought I would live to tell. Not letting fear run my life is still a struggle. There are parts of my life that I am ashamed of; parts that I don't really want to remember or acknowledge. What I have discovered is that for every part of me I try to keep hidden away, a good part of me is lost. With every embarrassing behavior, there is also a hidden talent or goodness. The Lord has seen fit to bring all things to my remembrance that I may learn how to be whole—that no part of me is lost and that I may be more free to exercise my agency.

No one else has power over who we will be. They can take away our freedom, they can torture, maim, and even kill, but they cannot take away our agency to determine what we will do with what we have been given. We cannot choose our circumstances or even our experiences, but we *can* choose who we will be. I have learned that if no pain is really what I wanted, I could have it. However, I have also learned that asking for a life with little or no pain is not asking for much at all. It is through those experiences that we can learn and grow and ultimately feel true joy.

> *No one else has power over who we will be.*

The ability to move on is always there, and if I look closely, a path opens up, inviting me forward. Each life-altering event has its own pain that needs to be healed or miracle to be accepted. Throughout my life, powerful experiences of feeling God's love through the kindness of others touched my heart. These are the moments I built my life on—the times that gave me life-saving hope.

Holding on to life and hope has finally brought me to the place I only dreamed of as a child. Instead of birthdays filled with fear, there are celebrations of life filled with love from Eric, our children, and grandchildren. I'm grateful to have eyes that are open to my successes in the past and the opportunity for continued growth in the years ahead. There is still sadness in looking back at my childhood and the loss of my innocence. However, in the aftermath of the storms, the light penetrates the dark and exposes the beauty of the journey that is my life.

SECTION TWO

SHEDDING LIGHT

CHAPTER 17

A HUSBAND'S PERSPECTIVE

This book was an incredible undertaking for Tammy to write. It was a labor of love that has spanned several years, multiple rewrites, and long instances of writer's blocks, but these were by far not the most difficult aspects of this project. Every time she wrote of or uncovered the secrets of what happened, a whole new box of fears and terror would open up and have to be dealt with. In the case of repressed memories, the intense fear and the memory of the event are all boxed up together until the victim is able to deal with the reality of the horrific event at a later date. These boxes are a normal part of what victims of abuse must delve into in order to expose the horrors of what transpired at the hands of the psychopaths that inflicted such pain.

What she has written here is only a very small sliver of the abuse that happened.

During the victimization, the perpetrators use threats, fear, and trauma in order to isolate their victims. They make sure that their victims will always be smaller or physically weaker than them. They excel in taking away a victim's sense of hope. When Tammy uncovered a new episode of repressed memory or feeling, she would have to get past the programmed repressed fear as well. This took incredible amounts of faith and strength—and time.

In writing about all this, it was especially difficult for her to show the horror of it without totally casting the reader into a dark pit. What she has written here is only a very small sliver of the abuse that happened. She has been determined not to let the darkness overshadow the light in her writings.

I was there for a large part of the story. Not that I was there for the first eighteen years of her life, but I have been there for the rest of her life so far. She has continued to amaze me in more ways than I could ever count.

Early on, when she first decided to write of her experiences and story, Tammy asked me to share a family member's perspective of the healing process. The hope is to help a victim's friends or family during their own journey. I am happy to share the things that I saw and learned along the way. As a sounding board and trusted confidant, I was a very large part of what transpired. Because the hurt was so extensive and horrific, Tammy leaned on me as well as others consistently for a period of several years.

There were many times when I failed in trying to give the comfort she needed, but I would usually try to do my best to listen, and I never doubted the truth of what she had to deal with. To me, the truth was painfully obvious. I am writing my perspective here on what I learned as a result. I am in no way a professional on human behavior, but I have spent a lot of time and energy trying to make sense of the actions of others.

Tammy and I first met at college when she was eighteen and I was seventeen. We began dating seriously not long after. Despite our young ages, we fell hopelessly in love and were married a year after we first met. We settled down, bought a little house, and started raising a family. Life, at times, was difficult with paying bills and taking care of the babies that soon came along. Over time, the houses got larger as our family grew. I thought we had this, but little did I know the wild ride we were soon to take.

Looking back now, I think, *How did I not know?* I knew Tammy's parents and had limited interactions with them. I must admit, when I found out about what had happened and what was still going on at the time, I really began questioning my intelligence level. I always thought I had normal intelligence, but the lack of awareness left me feeling stupid and inadequate. I had so much trust and confidence in my and Tammy's relationship, I didn't think anything could ever come between us. Not understanding how memory repression and PTSD worked, it was indeed a hard pill for me to swallow to learn that there was a whole other part of her life that I, as well as she, didn't have the slightest idea about.

Early on, we both decided that what we had to deal with had to have a sufficient purpose. She could never be asked to deal with all the trauma and pain without a reason. To say it all didn't matter or was just simply "too bad" was not going to suffice for either of us. Justice in the face of all the horror demanded we have our answers. I *demanded* we have those answers—and they did come. The inspiration we received made the whole experience, in the end, a very harsh but incredible journey.

Two of the biggest questions I needed to have answered were "how?" and "why?" Specifically, *how* could people do these things seemingly under everybody's noses without them knowing, and *why* would they even want to? (I'm sure you are probably asking these same questions yourself.) It took a while for the first answer to be formulated, (remember, average intelligence) and the answer to the second question I found out in the most demeaning of all places.

In the case of *how* it happened, you must realize that the abuse was systematic and usually planned out. Not always, but

> *Two of the biggest questions I needed to have answered were "how?" and "why?"*

usually. Those that were responsible were very well-trained and much of it occurred in a ritualistic cult setting. Tammy talked about her dad's "family bible," which was actually a "how to" book of training for those who feel the need to victimize. This book had been passed down from generation to generation.

What they are really doing is traumatizing their young victims to the point of creating PTSD and causing them to disassociate from the memories. This is a well-known process among some of today's leading mental health care professionals. The next day, the victim seems to be normal and responsive, leaving the victimizer to believe they have some sort of "special power" given to them by the powers that be or whoever they are worshiping at the time. This feeling of invincibility spills over to other interactions with the victim. Another thing I had to learn is the amount of manipulation these people use. They have it down to an art. Cunning and deceptive, they can change their persona in a heartbeat to use in any circumstance.

The reality is that all they have done is tap into a God-given protection possessed by the victim to disassociate. What the abuser doesn't know or see is that at the time of the abuse, everything they have done has been recorded down to the most minute detail by the victim. It was amazing to me when Tammy would have recall: she could remember smells and peoples' clothing and places with exacting detail. After we had her dad arrested, during the investigation, she was able to identify victims from old photographs, as well as lead the investigators to ritual altar sites despite those sites being in faraway states. The things recorded in her brain happened sometimes as much as twenty-five years earlier, yet they were still very fresh in her mind.

During her dad's pretrial it was very interesting and gratifying to see the effect on him as the district attorney and Tammy's psychologist explained how PTSD works and how the victims still very much have a memory of what happened. They explained that, many times, the victims will begin to recall the abuse later—when they are in an emotionally safe setting. Tammy's dad's whole life was crashing down before him as each revelation coming from those experts—as well as from Tammy and her siblings—gained momentum. He began to slink down in his defendant's seat, lower and lower, until at the end of their testimony, his head was barely seen over the chair he was sitting on. His lifelong "religion," along with all its attributes (including protections), had been totally explained away in the space of a few short hours. He saw that there would be a reckoning at some level for all his wicked crimes.

In the case of "why?" people do these things, answers came from the most unlikely of places: a maximum-security prison. A childhood friend of mine, Al, had been incarcerated there for several years for arson. I made it a point to go visit him, usually once a month. I learned a lot from those visits and felt that they may have been of some benefit to him. Al was normally a very carefree and kind person, always fun to be around. In prison, he acted entirely differently as a form of self-preservation. One day, he told me a story of an incident he had in his cell. It's important to know that my friend was all of 5'6" and weighed probably 145 pounds. The telling of the story went something like this:

"They gave me a new cellmate." Al paused.

"He was a real big guy, over 300 pounds and trying to act all tough." Al was looking at me intently now.

"We got in a fist fight; I beat the crap out of him." Al was waiting to see my reaction.

"It was kind of expected of me. He's a child molester, you know, *one of the weak ones.*" Al said this last sentence so matter-of-factly.

Pieces to the puzzle I had been looking for started to fit. I had just found an enormous part of the answer I had been looking for. The *"why?"* was a total, pathetic weakness on the part of the abuser. I looked around at the prisoners that were there on visiting day and listened to some of them blaming others and complaining about their condition. I could see a lot of weakness. In all of the social mess prison life is, the absolute weakest of the weak, those most despised and at the bottom of the barrel in the hierarchy of the whole institution were those that molested children. They were looked down on, even by arsonists, murderers, and thieves.

To hurt others simply for pleasure is so foreign to how I think, believe, and how I was brought up. I firmly believe most people feel the same way. To do such evil things goes against most people's nature. Because they don't understand it, many people would rather not believe such things exist. I don't blame them. It's not a part of humanity many of us like to look at. However, to turn a blind eye to it or to attack the victim's integrity is to play a fool's part in a very important aspect of what goes on in our earthly existence. Abusers use unsuspecting people's naivety to their benefit to carry out their horrific plans. I'm sorry to say, something I learned early on is how easy it is for them to fool unsuspecting, decent people (especially caring family members). It even gives them a greater sense of superiority.

I now understand abusers are the *weakest of the weak.* These people crave to have a sense of power. They don't care how or what form it takes, the feeling of overpowering another person (no matter how small or weak) or thing (animal) gives them what they crave. Even babies are very much at risk. Abusers look scary and powerful to their victims because they will always make sure they have complete control of the setting. To act on such feelings would be seen as cowardice and reprehensible by those of us with normal inclinations, but abusers don't care, they only want to feel in control—to have that false sense of empowerment. They will take it any way they can get it. They only see their victims as a means to an end. Are they narcissistic? Absolutely. Again, I add, it is so hard for decent people to see or understand this behavior.

> *I now understand abusers are the weakest of the weak.*

Once an abuser acts to victimize those that are weaker, I believe they have crossed over a line. It is said that the feeling of power to a weak person that victimizes others can be intoxicating. No amount of it is enough. What I learned is that they can't see themselves in the bad light of their actions, so they start piecing together an alternative reality, one in which they aren't responsible for their actions. Every time I've had to deal with abusive people, it was very apparent to me they had their own pseudo-reality. Others, or situations, are blamed instead of looking inward. To me, they become animalistic. They live to experience a false sense of power and feel important. They think they are fooling the world (including God himself), all the while not being able to see how their own lives have become a cesspool.

Tammy's parents thought they had it all: riches, looks, and power. All I saw was ugly people living in squalor and ignorance.

It didn't matter to them. They were manufacturing their own reality. To me, it looked like what I call self-retardation, because *they couldn't see that the ones they were fooling the most were themselves.* I would say they were living ineffectual lives except for one thing: they had the ability to cause a great amount of pain and suffering. People who don't live in reality can be capable of almost any deed, no matter how horrific or sick. In their world, there is no responsibility or repercussions for actions. If you in some way invite them into the real world, it will only cause them to see you as an enemy.

It's interesting to see that although Tammy had been severely weakened by her own abuse and living in such a dysfunctional home, she was motivated to take a different path to attain the things she wanted for a better life.

> *People who don't live in reality can be capable of almost any deed, no matter how horrific or sick.*

How Tammy came out of such a situation and built a good life for herself is a great lesson in the God-given gift of free agency—the ability to act for oneself independently of external situations. Her parents worked night and day to make her like them. In the end, they failed. Yes, they caused her a tremendous amount of suffering and every kind of pain one could imagine; they didn't fail due to a lack of incredible effort on their part. I believe what most angered them about her was the inner strength she maintained. She was a constant reminder of how their failures were theirs and theirs alone to bear. She took away their excuses and eventually tore down some of their fake façade. When people like them are confronted with any reality, I get the image of the weeping and wailing and gnashing of teeth during judgment that we read about in the Bible.[8]

One of the first things Tammy and I did when the truths of her upbringing started coming out was to stop all communication with her father. Later, when the much harder truths about her mother surfaced, we also stopped all contact with her. It seemed it wasn't hard for them. When they saw that the gig was up, they knew that they had to move on to other places and people. They can't be around those that know the truths they were trying to hide from others and themselves.

Stopping all contact with them was a big help in Tammy starting to heal. Sadly, when her sisters (who also knew of the abuse) refused to acknowledge the extent of their parents' guilt, we realized Tammy also would have to stop communication with them. Her well-being and ability to heal was at risk. Anyone who isn't willing to acknowledge the truths of their family members or others in these situations will never be able to fully heal, especially if contact is continued. Too many victims will try to manufacture their own semi-reality to avoid the full extent of the pain they suffered. They will eventually attempt to derail those that are trying to deal with the full ramifications of abuse.

When the truths Tammy was exposing of the horrific conditions she had been subjected to during and after her upbringing surfaced, I would look at her and at the life she and I had worked so hard to build. I could see how she had affected others (as well as myself) for good. There were so many positive things in her life, and I would constantly ask her how she could possibly get from there to *here?* One of the reasons I had been fooled by her parents was because I could never imagine that someone as good as her could have come from such despicable people. At first, Tammy said she didn't know how she had built such a meaningful life despite all of the abuse, but slowly, the answers to that question started to come forward.

One of the things that quickly became apparent to me was how hard Tammy was willing to work to have a decent life. She wanted a nice, loving family, complete with a loving husband and, by God, that was what she was going to have! She was willing to scratch and claw her way to the goals she had set for herself at an early age. Most of those goals she could see had been reached by others outside of her family's sphere of influence. Tammy looked upon their good examples with longing eyes and took the steps she thought were necessary to accomplish them.

When she was away from the bad examples of her parents (and others), she started making *good* choices that would eventually get her where she wanted to be. She had learned at some level what she didn't want. One of the things I quickly learned from dealing with all of this is that where we end up in life isn't entirely based on where we started from but rather where our choices have taken us. I admit, there are a lot of things that happen that are out of our control in life, but we will always have decisions to make. Tammy has shown me that making good decisions will lead us to a very positive end.

Not that it was easy for her. She had to start from scratch with a very shaky foundation. If you can, imagine growing up in a family where good was seen as bad and bad portrayed as good, where a child isn't taught strength and how to overcome. Instead, she was taught to give in to evil means to gain something. They taught her that she was worthless and less than everybody else, that she was chattel, there only for their evil whims and desires. She had to overcome obstacles far worse than I or most other people had as part of our growing up. She built her life from far *less* than nothing. I believe others have had to overcome these same types of obstacles and they deserve a huge amount of respect. They stand as a testimony of God's true power in the face of the evilest of people's intentions or difficult situations. It's people's noble actions in the face of fear and rejection that shows the most incredible examples of humanity. That is *true* empowerment.

> *One of the things I quickly learned from dealing with all of this is that where we end up in life isn't entirely based on where we started from but rather where our choices have taken us.*

I have heard so many people's assessment of abusive or heinous situations as proof that there is no God, or at the very least that he doesn't care. We found the truth to be far different. When the facts of her situation started to engulf both of us, we

saw that the only way forward was to rely on faith and the healing power of the Savior. To stray from that knowledge only led
to despair and a far more weakened state. *Faith led us to strength
and the ability to overcome.*

It would have been easy to look toward an easier outcome,
one in which God in his power would send down lightning and
thunderbolts to burn the evil people to quivering crisps. I must
admit, it does sound like a fitting and just end. Having now
somewhat come out the other side (it's still an ongoing process),
though, we can see the reasoning of a just and perfect God. Evil
people will use their God-given gift of free agency (the ability
to steer our own course in this life) to their own enslavement
and downfall. Others who use the same gift to lift up themselves
and others can accomplish exceptional feats and progress to an
incredible height, especially in the face of adversity. It is up to
us to decide, and God will not take this gift away. It is so very
important to God and his work of our eternal progression.

Evil people will never believe in this gift. In Tammy's case, and
many others (where God knew he couldn't interfere with man's
agency), he put protections in place. PTSD and dissociation may
look like a high price to pay, but it can allow the victims to move
forward. Tammy now says that it was this protection that allowed
her to move toward the accomplishments in her life. Her own
free agency was protected. Dealing with the horror of it all at a
later date is what has defined much of her life and given it a far
greater purpose. In helping her deal with this, I also learned
incredible truths that have helped me in my progress, both on
a personal and a professional level. It was hard, but we both feel
blessed in countless ways as a result. Our Heavenly Father did
not abandon us.

Tammy today is a very well-adjusted and wonderful person.
Despite all that she has been through, I must admit she is one
of the most realistic people I know. She is beautiful and full of
life and is loved by virtually all who come in contact with her.
She is a devoted and loving wife, mother, and grandmother who
will forever be a part of our lives in a good, wholesome way. She

makes me give her lots of hugs and kisses, which is a small price to pay to help her feel loved and accepted. She says that she has everything she ever wanted and then some. A lot was stolen from her by demented people; regardless, she has managed to turn such a hopeless condition into a life full of light and wonder.

Our Heavenly Father did not abandon us.

Tammy must work hard on her emotional well-being every day to continue in her progress. She still bears some of the physical scars from the abuse, but they serve as a testament to all she has and will continue to overcome. I have to say, without a doubt, she is the strongest and most incredible person I have ever met.

— "Eric"

HEALING TRUTHS

TO SURVIVORS OF ABUSE
—A NOTE FROM TAMMY

When you have been a victim of any kind of abuse, one of the hardest things to do is to admit to yourself and others that you have been deeply hurt by those who should love and care for you. Whether you are an abused child or adult, the feelings of helplessness and fear you experience can be devastating. The truths listed here are not an easy fix, but can help sustain us through the rocky parts of the journey.

- The pain that comes from abuse can lead to denying or minimizing the abuse. Pretending that the pain or abuse itself does not exist only enables the abuser's destructive influence to continue and retains us as victims. We cannot overcome the effects of the abuse if we are not willing to accept the reality of it and deal with its full effects. No matter what anyone says, we *did not* and *do not* deserve the pain we have suffered at the hands of our abusers.
- Facing the truths of our pain is never as easy as others may say it should be. The intensity of the fear and powerlessness that accompany the pain affect our confidence in moving forward and sometimes cloud our ability to see our life's worth. Letting the pain out in productive ways—crying, writing, talking, etc.—frees us from its stranglehold and the self-destructive behaviors

that would destroy us. Processing the pain also allows us to internalize the strengthening emotions of joy, peace, and love. Your life *can* be filled with light and hope. You were *meant* to find happiness in this life.

- Seeking help is not an admission of failure, but acceptance of the complexity of what we have been through. There are many healing paths and professionals to help. We don't have to do this alone.

- Every abuser needs help and healing of their own, but the victim is *never* the one to give it. As a victim, the best thing you can do for the abuser and yourself is to leave them to the care of those who are trained to help and move forward on your own path.

- Forgiveness is a healing part of the journey when seen simply as an intentional decision to let go of anger, vengeance, or resentment. Forgiveness does *not* mean it is okay that the abuse happened. It does *not* mean a renewed or continued relationship with the abuser. Forgiveness is part of the process of dismantling the chains that the abuser would have you wear.

- Being abused does not take away who we are. We are not weak, but gifted and capable. We cannot change the past and we can't ignore it, but we can learn from it. We have the ability to choose what we will do and where we will go from this point forward.

- Step 2 of the Alcoholics Anonymous recovery program is about accepting a higher power or that there is a power greater than ourselves. It's about being humble enough to accept we need help and is a healing principle. Believing and trusting in something good and more powerful than ourselves can fill the voids and help let down the walls that keep us from feeling joy. It opens our eyes to paths of healing.

TO FRIENDS OF ABUSE VICTIMS
—A NOTE FROM TAMMY

Childhood abuse resulted in most of my energy being used to fight feelings of worthlessness and despair. At one of my lowest points as a teenager, a leader in our youth group reached out to me for help with a project. Her "needing" me planted a seed of hope—maybe there was something inside me of value. That seed led to healing truths as I continued to reach for a better life. If you know someone who is facing the trauma of abuse, here are several things to keep in mind:

- A compassionate listener is of great worth to a grieving heart. You don't need to solve their problems, but simply support them as they seek out the solutions.
- Be patient in the recovery process—it is a *process*.
- *Never* minimize the deep extent of the effects of the trauma they suffered. Although the abuse may have happened far in the past, it can still have a dramatic effect on their present.
- See their worth and invite them to share their gifts and talents.
- Know your own boundaries and be gentle and firm in setting them.
- You can't fix them and you both need to know that. Reassure them in believing in their own abilities to find healing and encourage them in seeking professional help.
- Acknowledging a Higher Power can be a great comfort to you as well as them. "Trust the Lord with all your heart and lean not on your own understanding."[9]

IF YOU OR SOMEONE YOU KNOW IS EXPERIENCING ABUSE, HELP IS AVAILABLE

Childhelp National Child Abuse Hotline
Professional crisis counselors are available 24 hours a day, 7 days a week, in over 170 languages. All calls are confidential. The hotline offers crisis intervention, information, and referrals to thousands of emergency, social service, and support resources.

Call or text 800-4-A-CHILD (800-422-4453)

Center for Missing and Exploited Children CyberTipline
Provides information about how to report online sexual exploitation of a child or if you suspect that a child has been inappropriately contacted online. Information will be made available to law enforcement to investigate.

Call 800-843-5678

National Domestic Violence Hotline
Hours: 24/7. Languages: English, Spanish, and 200+ through interpretation service

Call 800-799-7233 or text START to 88788

Thehotline.org

Suicide and Crisis Lifeline
Hours: Available 24 hours. Languages: English, Spanish.

SMS: 988

You can also reach the Crisis Text Line by texting MHA to 741741. You can also call 1-800-985-5990 or text "TalkWithUs" to 66746 at the SAMHSA Disaster Distress Helpline.

988lifeline.org

ENDNOTES

1. Name Withheld, "A Refuge for the Oppressed," January 1, 1992. https://www.churchofjesuschrist.org/study/ensign/1992/01/a-refuge-for-the-oppressed?lang=eng.

2. Samuel Medley, "I Know That My Redeemer Lives," *Hymns*, no. 136.

3. "About." National 4-H Council, September 28, 2023. http://www.4-h.org/about/.

4. Exod. 20:12 (KJV)

5. Exod. 20:3-5 (KJV)

6. Matt. 18:21 (KJV)

7. Matt. 18:6 (KJV)

8. Matt. 13:43, 8:12 (KJV)

9. Prov. 3:5 (NIV)

REVIEW INQUIRY

Hey, it's Tammy here.

I hope you've enjoyed the book, finding it both informative and encouraging. I have a favor to ask you.

Would you consider giving it a rating wherever you bought the book? Online book stores are more likely to promote a book when they feel good about its content, and reader reviews are a great barometer for a book's quality.

Please go to the website of wherever you bought the book, search for my name and the book title, and leave a review. If able, perhaps consider adding a picture of you holding the book. That increases the likelihood your review will be accepted!

Many thanks in advance,

Tammy René

WILL YOU SHARE THE LOVE?

Get this book for a friend, associate, or family member!

If you have found this book valuable and know others who would find it useful, consider buying them a copy as a gift. Special bulk discounts are available if you would like your reading group or organization to benefit from reading this. Just contact 915tammy@gmail.com or visit https://buildonthelight.com/.

WOULD YOU LIKE TAMMY RENÉ TO SPEAK TO YOUR ORGANIZATION?

Book Tammy Now!

Tammy René accepts a limited number of speaking engagements each year. To learn how you can bring her message of hope to your organization, email 915tammy@gmail.com or visit https://buildonthelight.com.

ABOUT THE AUTHOR

Tammy René passionately shares messages of hope and healing. A survivor of childhood sexual and physical abuse in a cult, Tammy navigated a path toward recovery, finding strength in her faith.

Most of the pain and heartache she has experienced came from the abuse she suffered at the hands of the very people who should have loved and protected her—her parents. When she was in her thirties, the full effects of the abuse crashed into the present, threatening to destroy the life she and her husband were building together. The following diagnoses of PTSD and Dissociative Identity Disorder forced her to admit she needed both help and answers. In the years that followed, she found wholeness and continued healing through regular therapy, writing, finding ways to encourage others, and holding onto the faith that is her lifeline.

"My journey has been about the freedom of learning and accepting truth. Even more importantly it is about rediscovering the light inside me and learning to own it, build on it, and share it. As we are willing to face the reality of the damage that the heartache caused, we find life-saving light that keeps the trauma from completely engulfing us."

She's worked as a CASA (Court Appointed Special Advocate) for abused and neglected children, currently volunteering with her local Suicide Prevention Network as a PTSD support group facilitator. She's a speaker, sharing her story to inspire hope in abuse victims and bring understanding to their communities. She is loving life in rural Nevada, cherishing time with her husband, children, and grandchildren.

Connect with Tammy at: https://buildonthelight.com